The Selected Poems of
FEDERICO GARCÍA
LORCA

The Selected Poems of
FEDERICO GARCÍA
LORCA

EDITED BY
Francisco García Lorca AND
Donald M. Allen

INTRODUCTION BY
W. S. Merwin

A NEW DIRECTIONS PAPERBOOK

Manufactured in the United States of America.
New Directions Books are printed on acid-free paper.
First published in a clothbound edition by New Directions in 1955;
first published as New Directions Paperbook 114 in 1961;
reissued, with an Introduction by W.S. Merwin, as New Directions Paperbook 1010 in 2005.
Published simultaneously in Canada by Penguin Books Canada Limited.
Book design by Sylvia Frezzolini Severance.

Library of Congress Cataloging-in-Publication Data

García Lorca, Federico, 1898–1936.
    [Poems. English & Spanish. Selections]
    The selected poems of Federico García Lorca / edited by
Francisco García Lorca and Donald M. Allen ;
introduction by W.S. Merwin.
        p. cm.
    Includes index.
    "New Directions book."
        ISBN 0-8112-1622-5 (alk. paper)
    1. García Lorca, Federico, 1898–1936. I. García Lorca, Francisco, 1902–
II. Allen, Donald Merriam, 1912-   III. Title.
    PQ6613.A763A223 2005
    861'.62—dc22

                                        2005002834

New Directions Books are published for James Laughlin
by New Directions Publishing Corporation,
80 Eighth Avenue, New York, NY 10011

CONTENTS

INTRODUCTION

by W. S. Merwin

Federico García Lorca was born a year and a half before the twentieth century and was murdered by the Falangists when he was thirty-eight. What he wrote in his short life made it impossible to imagine the poetry not only of Spain and the Spanish language everywhere, but of the whole Western world, since then, without him.

These unpredictable bursts of light occur in our history but they are not encountered, afterwards, in chronological order. Modern poetry began, for me, not in English at all but in Spanish, which I scarcely knew, in the poems of Lorca, and even more specifically in one book of his, the *Romancero Gitano* (*Gypsy Ballads*), which Lorca had finished in the year I was born, and with two poems in particular *La Casada Infiel* (*The Faithless Wife*) and *Romance Somnambulo* (*Somnambulist Ballad*). I was sixteen, in my first semester at college, drunk with Milton and Shelley, and continuing my years of high-school Spanish under the intense tutelage of a small, deeply homesick young assistant professor from Spain, Prof. Soria, a figure from Murillo, black beret pulled down all around his head. He arrived at class on a bicycle, propelled by his passion for the poetry, the plays, voice and radiance of Federico García Lorca, who had been killed just eight years before. Elements of his sustained excitement were contagious, even to someone whose textbook Spanish was as uncertain and tone-deaf as mine was. Before I had ever heard of Eliot or Pound I remember walking across the campus under the summer trees muttering under my breath

> *Y que yo me la llevé al rio*
> *creyendo que era mozuela,*
> *pero tenia marido.*

There were few translations of the poems at the time, as I recall. Prof. Soria, ardent, somber, and dedicated, was not interested in them in any case, and did not encourage his few students to look for any, but instead he urged us to make our own. I arrived at an English version of those hypnotic lines that went something like

And so I took her to the river
believing she was still a girl
but she had a husband.

That relayed the dictionary meaning of the lines, more or less, but the fire, the beat and snap and dance of the original had somehow evaporated on the way. I could hear that earlier life distinctly, and feel it, in the words of its own language, which I could scarcely speak, but for all my efforts I could not conjure up that sound and vitality, or even a distant echo of them, in English, and at the same time I had no doubt that they were what made it a poem. I could recognize their authoritative presence by then, when I came upon it in my own language. I knew it in the immense rolling splendors of *Paradise Lost* and *Samson Agonistes*, and in the occasional soaring flights of Shelley (that other singular voice cut short a century before Lorca's death, part of whose genius was his address to the skylark as a projection of his own spirit) and so I knew what I was listening for, what I needed to hear and to hear again.

That poem, indeed those few lines of Lorca's, written in his late twenties, introduced me to two unbounded realms. One of them was the no-man's land of translation itself, its desirability, in fact its necessity, and at the same time its impossibility, the interminable enterprise of trying to conjure up in one's own language a voice, an authority that would convey the life, the poetry of the original. But that lure, and the never-never land beyond it (for what we want translation to be is the very thing it can never be: the original) are a subject of their own. Those few lines led me also to the rest of Lorca's poetry, not as literature but—at its clearest and most assuredly his own—as enchantment, epiphany, presence. Lorca's poem led me to hear poetry, and to recognize it, in another language, and so to the discovery of the rich vein of modern poetry in Spanish, from Machado to Neruda—just by chance an older student who thought it might interest me gave me a copy of Neruda's *Residencia en la Tierra* (*Residence on Earth*) at almost the same time, which I found baffling and endlessly seductive. And because of Lorca it was the modern poets in Spanish who I read first, before I got around to the ballads, and to Quevedo and St. John of the Cross.

Lorca, from his childhood on, had been drawn, by his gifts and temperament, to the theater, to the theatrical, and he wrote a succession of plays that were celebrated in Spain during his lifetime, and they retain a significant place in his surviving work. In our young Spanish professor's love of Lorca (and in his own homesickness) the plays were one with the poems. He was trying to make a translation of *Las Bodas de Sangre* (*Blood Wedding*) and he got us to help him. His ardor for the plays swept me along at the time, and I became familiar with all of them. There was no opportunity to see any of them on a stage, of course.

In English, in performance, as I would come to see, Lorca's plays, in the theatrical context of the later twentieth century, were apt to seem exotic and remote. They embody conventions that are not only exclusively Spanish but are also exclusively Lorca's, descendants of his love of folk poetry, pageants, rituals, processions, popular legends and theater, and most of all dance, particularly the passions and drama of Andalusian gypsy dance and music. Lorca's brother, Francisco, in his book *In The Green Morning: Memories of Federico,* tells of how he and his brother, as children, invented stories together, and of how some of Federico's plays were suggested by popular poems, one of them at least by a few lines from a street ballad, something as common and as ephemeral in early twentieth-century Spain as latter-day comic books. He also describes one rehearsal of *Blood Wedding* that was done as a pantomime, without musical accompaniment and *without words* (p. 206, New Directions edition, 1980). The very possibility of that emphasizes the balletic quality of Lorca's drama, the broad, clear outlines of the characters, and their situations and action. From the beginning Lorca was envisaging a kind of theater far removed from the naturalism that followed Ibsen. Among its ancestry were the great poets of the theater of the Spanish Golden Age, and the poet-playwrights of Rome and Athens.

Transposing any part of Lorca's theatrical writing to another language, another culture and period, summons the perennial problems of translation, never solved with any finality. Some of the difficulties are obvious, and it may be the plays' character as ballets, and as heirs of popular pantomimes that survives most convincingly. It is the poems, above all, that have stayed before me, through the years since I first read them, and that I go on hearing. Among his writings they hold, in its purest form, the tone, the life, the presence, that I have been listening for from the beginning. Lorca had his own name for that. He called it *duende*, the demonic inspiration, something akin to what Nietzsche described as the Dionysian urge.

The idea of the *duende*, and the mystery that surrounds it, came to signify for Lorca the essence of what he hoped to be guided by and to give voice to in his poetry. He wrote about it directly in an exalted lecture, a kind of manifesto, *Juego y teoría del duende* (*Play and theory of the duende*), which he delivered in Buenos Aires on Oct. 20, 1933 (*In Search of Duende*, New Directions, 1998). The lecture was a great occasion, a high moment in a peak period of his life. A month later he and Pablo Neruda spoke and read together in public. The *duende* that Lorca invoked then and later was a name for the wild current that they were both holding. Lorca's devotion to it, and his testimony, came to signify the heart of his aspiration. What he understood by the word, its manifestations in his writings, in his comments and his life, and its kinships with other emanations of the Dionysian force, have been explored by those who have written about Lorca from the evening of his lecture to the present, most recently in a beautiful, wide-ranging essay by Ed Hirsch, *The Demon and the Angel* (Harcourt 2002). In view of other things that we know about Lorca and his sources it is not surprising that the word *duende*, and the idea of it, are rooted in the Spanish gypsy tradition. In the language of the Spanish Rom the word for this force, this presence, is *duquende*, a figure of anarchic magic, a spirit that may "possess" a singer or dancer. Its significance, in the arts and in life as a mysterious whole is an inexhaustible subject, and in Lorca's work it is crucial, and obviously not subject to any one neat configuration or explanations but a signatory presence. In his own essay, "Deep Song," he quotes a sentence of a famous gypsy singer, Manuel Torre: "All that has black sounds has *duende.*"

Four years before that lecture in Buenos Aires his *duende* had led him to New York City, in June 1929, bringing with him, on his first trip away from his native country, the vivid images and sounds of Andalusia and of the folk and gypsy culture, the beat of flamenco and dancing that had become part of his own pulse. He came to New York in the last, unhappy stages of a searing love affair with a younger man, a sculptor, who had not returned Lorca's passion but had made use of him for his own ambitions. The crisis was compounded by the fact that Spanish culture rejected and condemned homosexuality outright, and his sexual orientation was no secret. His nascent fame had spread the talk about it. There were crises in his friendships at that time as well, touched off by his growing reputation. Luis Buñuel, the filmmaker, who bad been a friend, disliked Lorca's use of gypsy culture, which he considered old hat and fake, and he worked to lure another of Lorca's artist friends, Salvador Dali, away from him. Lorca's reaction, the alienation that he felt, came to include an impatience with what he called (in a letter to José Antonio Rubio Sacristan, published in C. Maurer's edition of Lorca's *Poesias*, p. xiii) "the myth of my gypsiness." "The gypsies," he wrote, "are nothing but a theme." He wanted to cut loose, and New York gave him his first experience of somewhere foreign, his first glimpse of huge urban crowds and a democratic, uprooted populace as varied and restless as a kaleidoscope. He was ready, or so he thought, for something utterly different from all he had known, and yet it is not surprising that his response to it, fueled by the feelings he brought to it, was fierce and violent.

He wanted a new kind of poetry, or at least a whole new phase, something beyond what he called the "poetry of the imagination," which for him was represented by the high baroque verse of the Spanish Golden Age, above all that of Luis de Gongora. He was hoping for what he called "inspired" poetry, which would be marked by its presentation of the *hecho poetico*, or poetic fact, a new primal entity of words, a new presence with no analogical reference outside itself. (Or none, presumably, except some emotional experience in the reader which would allow for a degree of recognition and some kind of response.)

His aspiration took the form of a book of new poems called *Poet in New York*, a sequence so much of a piece that it is sometimes referred to as a single poem. Christopher Maurer, in his introduction to the 1988 Farrar Strauss Giroux bi-lingual edition, says that it is both "a condemnation of modern urban civilization—the spiritual emptiness epitomized by New York City—and a dark cry of metaphysical loneliness." Some seventy years after the poem was written, and after many books and essays have analyzed and commented on it, both aspects of it are obviously still there, but the work's surviving, indefinable power, its troubling and exhilarating eruption, its *duende*, reaches beyond both. The imagery is a step in the dark beyond anything in his earlier writing. It leaps out of itself as it goes. It is explosive, glittering, shrill, raucous, a deliberately strident echo and nightmarish reversal of Whitman's programmatic optimism. It has attracted both hostility and enthusiasm, and has been labeled surrealist, for whatever that may be worth, and condemned as hysterical, and it has also been hailed as a kind of prophetic book. Whatever one may read about this inflamed, incantatory, enigmatic work leads back—unless the reader becomes mired in commentary—to the fiery gusher itself that Lorca tapped in New York. *Poet In New York* remains one of the sources of dark radiation of its time, as painful and suggestive as when it was written, a matrix from which the fearful lava continues to flow.

Lorca did not stop there. After the meeting with Neruda in the early thirties he went back to Spain and wrote, besides his late plays, some of his most beautiful poems, in which the "theme" (as the Spanish gypsy view of the world had been the "theme" of his poems in the twenties) was the poetry of Arabic Spain. His *Gacelas* in the *Divan del Tamarit,* published in the same year that he was murdered, are not charged with the violence of *Poet in New York,* but their indissoluble images, their "poetic facts," emerge from unsounded depths and remain as radiant as anything he wrote. He had arrived once again at what still seems like a new beginning and it is impossible not to wonder where he might have gone. The present selection was made nearly twenty years after Lorca's death by Donald Allen and Lorca's brother Francisco to introduce Lorca's poetry to American readers.

2005

PREFACE

by Francisco García Lorca

In making the present selection from the whole of the published verse of Federico García Lorca,° the editors have sought to choose poems they consider to be most representative of the many very different facets of the poet's varied and complex work. The severe limitations of space imposed by the format of the *New Classics* series, together with the several obstacles in the way of successful translation of much of García Lorca's verse, have obliged them to omit a number of the poems they originally hoped to include. These factors are responsible for the most regrettable omission—the lyrics from the poet's plays. A more comprehensive volume should certainly include many verse passages from the drama.

At the same time, the editors believe that the present selection is the most comprehensive, varied, and complete attempted to date. While they regret the absence of some good translators and the meager representation of the work of others, they feel that nearly all the translations included are faithful to the text of the Spanish poems and, more often than not, to the spirit as well, insofar as this is possible in the incredibly difficult matter of translating poetry.

The *Libro de Poemas*, García Lorca's first published volume of poetry, included work that showed the greatest diversity in form, theme, and attitude. It is a book pregnant with themes, many of which were more fully developed in later books, while others died with the poet. A wider choice from this volume to illustrate more completely the vivid adolescent immaturity of a true poet would have forced the editors to sacrifice later poems that showed a greater maturity.

In *Canciones* the poet checks his first flights in order to achieve greater purification of the lyric. The atmosphere of transcendental romantic sensibility gives way to fleeting states of mind, momentary sensations, or a disinterested humor, often imbued with a note of elegiac

° A chronology of the poet's life is given on page 181

melancholy. A wide selection from the *Canciones* is included here because many critics have found that the poet attained the pinnacle of his lyricism in these poems.

From the *Cante Jondo* only one poem, *"La Saeta"* (the arrow), is included. The *"cante jondo"* (literally, "deep song") is a typically Andalusian sung lyric which critics contend comes from a very ancient tradition. They point to its peculiar structure, its melodic configuration, and the strange obsessive reiteration of a dominant note. In 1921, Manuel de Falla with García Lorca organized a competition to save this type of song from the vulgarization it had fallen into and the extinction which threatened it by giving it again the standards implied in its Andalusian heritage. *Saetas* are sung without guitar accompaniment while the images of Christ and the Virgin pass by in the Holy Week processions.

Of the eighteen ballads that make up the *Romancero Gitano*—García Lorca's most popular book—eight are included here. The ballad *(romance)* is a type of epico-lyric poem, which derives ultimately from the Spanish national epic. The old, traditional, anonymous, and popular ballad has grown with the spread of the language and has been nourished wherever Spanish was spoken. A series of great poets have enriched this unique type of Spanish poem, while remaining faithful to the essence of the tradition. In spite of its unchanging metrical structure, the *romance* has proven to be amazingly flexible in the hands of gifted poets and capable of expressing the most varied shades of sensibility. Exceptionally versatile, it is the poem of open fields and village squares, equally adaptable to the most exquisite baroque refinements, sung at time with simple, ancient, nostalgic melodies, or to the delicate measures of court music. Lope de Vega and Góngora used the *romance* in the seventeenth century, as did the Duque de Rivas and Zorrilla in the romantic period, and many modem poets. In his *Romancero Gitano* García Lorca returned to the epic tradition of the *romance* and enriched the form with vivid new interpretations.

Most of *Poeta en Nueva York* was composed while the poet was in residence at Columbia University during the depression of 1929-1930. These poems reveal the shock and anguish García Lorca experienced as he, the representative of a traditional culture, was confronted with the seeming chaos of a new industrial civilization. If one thing distinguished

Poeta en Nueva York from all his earlier books, it is the total absence of irony and humor: nourished by the "bitter root," these poems speak tragically and grotesquely on a prevailing desolation.

After his return to Spain, García Lorca wrote his greatest elegy: *Llanto por Ignacio Sánchez Mejías*—a formal lament for his friend, the famous bullfighter, who was killed in the bull ring at five o'clock in the afternoon. The restrained yet profound emotion, the vast and almost grandiose movement of its sad music, and the great complexity of its diverse elements—almost a synthesis of all the principal aspects of the poet's verse—these make the *Lament* one of García Lorca's very greatest achievements.

In the *Divan del Tamarit* he returned again to the shorter lyric. This work, never published in book form, was written in honor of the Arabic-Grenadine poets. The title is taken from two Arabic words: *divan* means a collection of poems, and *Tamarit* is the ancient name of a place near Granada where the poet's family owned a country house. It was there that most of this volume was written. The forms of the poems, too, owe something to the Arabic. Both the *casida* and the *gacela* are short, rhymed, fixed verse forms in Arabic poetry. García Lorca knew Arabic poetry only in translation, and his *casida* and *gacela* are free adaptations. There are, however, these similarities: the theme of the night visit which is frequent in Arabic poetry, certain chromatic images, and homage to the city as an object of love: a theme that passed into Spanish poetry from the Arabic. In this return to the shorter lyric forms there is implicit all the sublimated poetic experience of García Lorca.

The Spanish text has been collated with the manuscripts, where they exist, and with the first published editions.

This edition owes much to the thoroughness of Donald M. Allen in collecting translations, also to his critical judgment which has prevailed in all cases where several versions of the same poem were found. To him I want to express my deep gratitude.

Both of the editors regret that more of the work of well-known translators of García Lorca could not be included in the present volume. They wish, too, that other good translators might have been represented. These and other omissions they hope to rectify at a later date when a larger selection is undertaken. For the present, they wish to express their gratitude to Sr. Jaime Salinas for his fine help in the early stages of planning this volume. They are most grateful, too, to Mr. Edwin Honig for his kind assistance, and to Mr. Herbert Cahoon, Mrs. Harriet de Onís, and Mr. William Jay Smith for their generous advice. Our deep gratitude goes as well to the many other translators without whose fine work this volume would not have been possible.

1955

TRANSLATORS

Jaime de Angulo

Ben Belitt

Roy Campbell

J.L. Gili

Norman di Giovanni

Edwin Honig

Langston Hughes

Rolfe Humphries

Donald Jenks

Lysander Kemp

A. L. Lloyd

Lloyd Mallan

W. S. Merwin

Harriet de Onís

Stanley Read

William Jay Smith

Stephen Spender

Greville Texidor

FROM

LIBRO DE POEMAS

1921

EL LAGARTO VIEJO

En la agostada senda
he visto al buen lagarto
(gota de cocodrilo)
meditando.
Con su verde levita
de abate del diablo,
su talante correcto
y su cuello planchado,
tiene un aire muy triste
de viejo catedrático.
¡Esos ojos marchitos
de artista fracasado,
cómo miran la tarde
desmayada!

¿Es éste su paseo
crepuscular, amigo?
Usad bastón, ya estáis
muy viejo, Don Lagarto,
y los niños del pueblo
pueden daros un susto.
¿Qué buscáis en la senda,
filósofo cegato,
si el fantasma indeciso
de la tarde agosteña
ha roto el horizonte?

¿Buscáis la azul limosna
del cielo moribundo?
¿Un céntimo de estrella?

¿O acaso
estudiasteis un libro
de Lamartine, y os gustan
los trinos platerescos
de los pájaros?

THE OLD LIZARD

In the parched path
I have seen the good lizard
(one drop of crocodile)
meditating.
with his green frock-coat
of an abbot of the devil,
his correct bearing
and his stiff collar,
he has the sad air
of an old professor.
Those faded eyes
of a broken artist,
how they watch the afternoon
in dismay!

Is this, my friend,
your twilight constitutional?
Please use your cane,
you are very old, Mr. Lizard,
and the children of the village
may startle you.
What are you seeking in the path,
my near-sighted philosopher,
if the wavering phantasm
of the parched afternoon
has broken the horizon?

Are you seeking the blue alms
of the moribund heaven?
A penny of a star?

Or perhaps
you've been reading a volume
of Lamartine, and you relish
the plateresque trills
of the birds?

(Miras al sol poniente,
y tus ojos relucen,
¡oh, dragón de las ranas!,
con un fulgor humano.
Las góndolas sin remos
de las ideas, cruzan
el agua tenebrosa
de tus iris quemados.)

¿Venís quizá en la busca
de la bella lagarta,
verde como los trigos
de Mayo,
como las cabelleras
de las fuentes dormidas,
que os despreciaba, y luego
se fué de vuestro campo?
¡Oh, dulce idilio roto
sobre la fresca juncia!
¡Pero vivir! ¡qué diantre!
me habéis sido simpático.
El lema de "me opongo
a la serpiente" triunfa
en esa gran papada
de arzobispo cristiano.

Ya se ha disuelto el sol
en la copa del monte,
y enturbian el camino
los rebaños.
Es hora de marcharse,
dejad la angosta senda
y no continuéis
meditando.
Que lugar tendréis luego
de mirar las estrellas
cuando os coman sin prisa
los gusanos.

(You watch the setting sun,
and your eyes shine,
oh, dragon of the frogs,
with a human radiance.
Ideas, gondolas without oars,
cross the shadowy
waters of your
burnt-out eyes.)

Have you come looking
for that lovely lady lizard,
green as the wheatfields
of May,
as the long locks
of sleeping pools,
who scorned you, and then
left you in your field?
Oh, sweet idyll, broken
among the sweet sedges!
But, live! What the devil!
I like you.
The motto "I oppose
the serpent" triumphs
in that grand double chin
of a Christian archbishop.

Now the sun has dissolved
in the cup of the mountains,
and the flocks
cloud the roadway.
It is the hour to depart:
leave the dry path
and your meditations.
You will have time
to look at the stars
when the worms are eating you
at their leisure.

¡Volved a vuestra casa
bajo el pueblo de grillos!
¡Buenas noches, amigo
Don Lagarto!

Ya está el campo sin gente,
los montes apagados
y el camino desierto;
sólo de cuando en cuando
canta un cuco en la umbría
de los álamos.

BALADA DE LA PLACETA

Cantan los niños
en la noche quieta;
¡arroyo claro,
fuente serena!

    LOS NIÑOS
¿Qué tiene tu divino
corazón en fiesta?

    YO
Un doblar de campanas
perdidas en la niebla.

    LOS NIÑOS
Ya nos dejas cantando
en la plazuela.
¡Arroyo claro,
fuente serena!

¿Qué tienes en tus manos
de primavera?

Go home to your house
by the village of the crickets!
Good night, my friend
Mr. Lizard!

Now the field is empty,
the mountains dim,
the roadway deserted.
Only, now and again,
a cuckoo sings in the darkness
of the poplar trees.

LYSANDER KEMP

BALLAD OF THE LITTLE SQUARE

The children sing
in the quiet night;
clear stream,
serene fountain!

THE CHILDREN
What joy does your divine
heart celebrate?

MYSELF
A clanging of bells
lost in the mist.

THE CHILDREN
You leave us singing
in the little square.
Clear stream,
serene fountain!

What signs of spring
do you hold in your hand?

YO
Una rosa de sangre
y una azucena.

LOS NIÑOS
Mójalas en el agua
de la canción añeja.
¡Arroyo claro,
fuente serena!

¿Qué sientes en tu boca
roja y sedienta?

YO
El sabor de los huesos
de mi gran calavera.

LOS NIÑOS
Bebe el agua tranquila
de la canción añeja.
¡Arroyo claro,
fuente serena!

¿Poz qué te vas tan lejos
de la plazuela?

YO
¡Voy en busca de magos
y de princesas!

LOS NIÑOS
¿Quién te enseñó el camino
de los poetas?

YO
La fuente y el arroyo
de la canción añeja.

MYSELF
A rose of blood
and a white lily.

THE CHILDREN
Dip them in the water
of the antique song.
Clear stream,
serene fountain!

What do you feel in your mouth
scarlet and thirsting?

MYSELF
The savour of the bones
of my great skull.

THE CHILDREN
Drink the tranquil water
of the antique song.
Clear stream,
serene fountain!

Why do you go so far
from the little square?

MYSELF
I go in search of magicians
and of princesses!

THE CHILDREN
Who showed you the path
of the poets?

MYSELF
The fountain and the stream
of the antique song.

LOS NIÑOS
¿Te vas lejos, muy lejos
del mar y de la tierra?

YO
Se ha llenado de luces
mi corazón de seda,
de campanas perdidas,
de lirios y de abejas.
Y yo me iré muy lejos,
más allá de esas sierras,
más allá de los mares,
cerca de las estrellas,
para pedirle a Cristo
Señor que me devuelva
mi alma antigua de niño,
madura de leyendas,
con el gorro de plumas
y el sable de madera.

LOS NIÑOS
Ya nos dejas cantando
en la plazuela,
¡arroyo claro,
fuente serena!

Las pupilas enormes
de las frondas resecas,
heridas por el viento,
lloran las hojas muertas.

THE CHILDREN
Do you go far, very far
from the sea and the earth?

MYSELF
My heart of silk
is filled with lights,
with lost bells,
with lilies and bees.
I will go very far,
farther than those hills,
farther than the seas,
close to the stars,
to beg Christ the Lord
to give back the soul I had
of old, when I was a child,
ripened with legends,
with a feathered cap
and a wooden sword.

THE CHILDREN
You leave us singing
in the little square,
clear stream,
serene fountain!

The enormous pupils
of the parched fronds
injured by the wind,
the dead leaves weep.

STEPHEN SPENDER
AND J. L. GILI

EL CONCIERTO INTERRUMPIDO

Ha roto la armonía
de la noche profunda,
el calderón helado y soñoliento
de la media luna.

Las acequias protestan sordamente
arropadas con juncias,
y las ranas, muecines de la sombra,
se han quedado mudas.

En la vieja taberna del problado
cesó la triste música,
y ha puesto la sordina a su aristón
la estrella más antigua.

El viento se ha sentado en los torcales
de la montaña oscura,
y un chopo solitario —el Pitágoras
de la casta llanura —
quiere dar con su mano centenaria,
un cachete a la luna.

LA BALADA DEL AGUA DEL MAR

El mar
sonríe a lo lejos.
Dientes de espuma,
labios de cielo.

—¿Qué vendes, oh joven turbia,
con los senos al aire?

THE INTERRUPTED CONCERT

The frozen sleepy pause
of the half moon
has broken the harmony
of the deep night.

The ditches, shrouded in sedge,
protest in silence,
and the frogs, muezzins of shadow,
have fallen silent.

In the old village inn
the sad music has ceased,
and the most ancient of stars
has muted its ray.

The wind has come to rest
in dark mountain caves,
and a solitary poplar — Pythagoras
of the pure plain —
lifts its aged hand
to strike at the moon.

                                   W. S. MERWIN

BALLAD OF THE WATER OF THE SEA

The sea
smiles from far off.
Teeth of foam,
lips of sky.

What do you sell, oh, turbid maid,
with your breasts to the wind?

—Vendo, señor, el agua
de los mares.

—Qué llevas, oh negro joven,
mezclado con tu sangre?

—Llevo, señor, el agua
de los mares.

—¿Esas lágrimas salobres
de dónde vienen, madre?

—Lloro, señor, el agua
de los mares.

—Corazón; y esta amargura
seria, ¿de dónde nace?

—¡Amarga mucho el agua
de los mares.

El mar
sonríe a lo lejos.
Dientes de espuma,
labios de cielo.

I sell, sir, the water
of the seas.

What do you carry, oh, black youth,
mixed with your blood?

I carry, sir, the water
of the seas

These salt tears,
Mother, from where do they come?

I weep, sir, the water
of the seas.

Heart; and this grave
bitterness, where was it born?

Very bitter is the water
of the seas!

The sea
smiles from far off.
Teeth of foam,
lips of sky.

LLOYD MALLAN

FROM

POEMA DEL CANTE JONDO

1921

POEMA DE LA SAETA

Arqueros

Los arqueros oscuros
a Sevilla se acercan.

Guadalquivir abierto.

Anchos sombreros grises
y largas capas lentas.

¡Ay, Guadalquivir!

Vienen de los remotos
países de la pena.

Guadalquivir abierto.

Y van a un laberinto.
Amor, cristal y piedra.

¡Ay, Guadalquivir!

Noche

Cirio, candil,
farol y luciérnaga.

La constelación
de la saeta.

Ventanitas de oro
tiemblan,
y en la aurora se mecen
cruces superpuestas.

POEM OF THE SAETA

Archers

The dark archers
approach Seville.

The open Guadalquivir.

Broad gray hats,
long slow cloaks.

Ay, Guadalquivir!

They come from remote
regions of sorrow.

The open Guadalquivir.

And they go to a labyrinth.
Love, crystal and rock.

Ay, Guadalquivir!

LYSANDER KEMP

Night

Candle, lamp,
lantern and firefly.

The constellation
of the dart.

Little windows of gold
trembling,
and cross upon cross
rocking in the dawn.

Cirio, candil,
farol y luciérnaga.

Sevilla

Sevilla es una torre
llena de arqueros finos.

Sevilla para herir.
Córdoba para morir.

Una ciudad que acecha
largos ritmos,
y los enrosca
como laberintos.
Como tallos de parra
encendidos.

¡Sevilla para herir!

Bajo el arco del cielo,
sobre su llano limpio,
dispara la constante
saeta de su río.

¡Córdoba para morir!

Y loca de horizonte,
mezcla en su vino
lo amargo de Don Juan
y lo perfecto de Dionisio.

Sevilla para herir.
¡Siempre Sevilla para herir!

Candle, lamp,
lantern and firefly.

JAIME DE ANGULO

Seville

Seville is a tower
full of fine archers.

Seville to wound.
Córdoba to die in.

A city that lurks
for long rhythms,
and twists them
like labyrinths.
Like tendrils of a vine
burning.

Seville to wound!

Under the arch of the sky,
across the clear plain,
she shoots the constant
arrow of her river.

Córdoba to die in!

And mad with horizons,
she mixes in her wine
the bitterness of Don Juan
and the perfection of Dionysus.

Seville to wound.
Always Seville to wound!

LYSANDER KEMP

Procesion

Por la calleja vienen
extraños unicornios.
¿De qué campo,
de qué bosque mitológico?
Más cerca,
ya parecen astrónomos.
Fantásticos Merlines
y el Ecce Homo,
Durandarte encantado.
Orlando furioso.

Paso

Virgen con miriñaque,
virgen de la Soledad,
abierta como un immenso
tulipán.
En tu barco de luces
vas
por la alta marea
de la ciudad,
entre saetas turbias
y estrellas de cristal.
Virgen con miriñaque,
tú vas
por el río de la calle,
¡hasta el mar!

Procession

Through the lanes
come strange unicorns.
From what fields,
from what mythological forest?
Nearer,
they look like astronomers.
Fantastic Merlins,
and the Ecce Homo.
Enchanted Durandarte.
Orlando Furioso.

LYSANDER KEMP

Paso

Virgin in crinoline,
Virgin of Solitude,
opened like an immense
tulip.
In your ship of lights
you go
  long the high tide
of the city,
among turbid saetas
and crystal stars.
Virgin in crinoline,
you go
down the river of the street
to the sea!

LYSANDER KEMP

23

Saeta

Cristo moreno
pasa
de lirio de Judea
a clavel de España.

¡Miradlo por dónde viene!

De España.
Cielo limpio y oscuro,
tierra tostada,
y cauces donde corre
muy lenta el agua.
Cristo moreno,
con las guedejas quemadas,
los pómulos salientes
y las pupilas blancas.

¡Miradlo por dónde va!

Balcon

La Lola
canta saetas.
Los toreritos
la rodean,
y el barberillo
desde su puerta,
sigue los ritmos
con la cabeza.
Entre la albahaca
y la hierbabuena,
la Lola canta
saetas.
La Lola aquella,

24

Arrow

Brown Christ
pass
from the lily of Judea
to the carnation of Spain.

Look where he comes!

From Spain.
Sky clear and dark,
parched land,
and watercourses where very
slowly runs the water.
Brown Christ,
with the burned forelocks,
the jutting cheekbones
and the white pupils.

Look where he goes!

W. S. MERWIN

Balcony

Lola
sings saetas.
The little bullfighters
circle around her
and the little barber,
from his doorway,
follows the rhythms
with his head.
Between the sweet basil
and the mint,
Lola sings
saetas.
That same Lola

que se miraba
tanto en la alberca.

Madrugada

Pero como el amor
los saeteros
están ciegos.

Sobre la noche verde
las saetas,
dejan rastros de lirio
caliente.

La quilla de la luna
rompe nubes moradas
y las aljabas
se llenan de rocío.

¡Ay, pero como el amor
los saeteros
están ciegos!

who looked so long
at herself in the pool.

W. S. MERWIN

Early Morning

But like love,
the archers
are blind.

Over the green night
the arrows
leave tracks of warm
lilies.

The keel of the moon
breaks purple clouds
and the quivers
fill with dew.

Ah, but like love,
the archers
are blind!

W. S. MERWIN

FROM

Primeras Canciones

1922

VARIACION

El remanso del aire
bajo la rama del eco.

El remanso del agua
bajo fronda de luceros.

El remanso de tu boca
bajo espesura de besos.

MEDIA LUNA

La luna va por el agua.
¡Cómo está el cielo tranquilo!
Va segando lentamente
el temblor viejo del río
mientras que una rana joven
la toma por espejito.

ADAN

Arbol de sangre moja la mañana
por donde gime la recién parida.
Su voz deja cristales en la herida
y un gráfico de hueso en la ventana.

Mientras la luz que viene fija y gana
blancas metas de fábula que olvida
el tumulto de venas en la huída
hacia el turbio frescor de la manzana,

VARIATIONS

The still waters of the air
under the bough of the echo.

The still waters of the water
under a frond of stars.

The still waters of your mouth
under a thicket of kisses.

LYSANDER KEMP

HALF MOON

The moon goes over the water.
How tranquil the sky is!
She goes scything slowly
the old shimmer from the river;
meanwhile a young frog
takes her for a little mirror.

W. S. MERWIN

ADAM

The morning by a tree of blood was dewed
and near to it the newborn woman groans.
Her voice left glass within the wound, and strewed
the window with a diagram of bones.

Meanwhile the day had reached with steady light
the limits of the fable, which evades
the tumult of the bloodstream in its flight
towards the dim cool apple in the shades.

Adán sueña en la fiebre de la arcilla
un niño que se acerca galopando
por el doble latir de su mejilla.

Pero otro Adán oscuro setá soñando
neutra luna de piedra sin semilla
donde el niño de luz se irá quemando.

CLARO DE RELOJ

Me senté
en un claro del tiempo.
Era un remanso
de silencio,
de un blanco silencio,
anillo formidable
donde los luceros
chocaban con los doce flotantes
números negros.

Adam, within the fever of the clay,
dreams a young child comes galloping his way,
felt in his cheeks, with double pulse of blood.

But a dark other Adam dreaming yearned
for a stone neuter moon, where no seeds bud,
in which that child of glory will be burned.

ROY CAMPBELL

PAUSE OF THE CLOCK

I sat down
in a space of time.
It was a backwater
of silence,
a white silence,
a formidable ring
wherein the stars
collided with the twelve floating
black numerals.

STANLEY READ

FROM

CANCIONES

1921–1924

NOCTURNO ESQUEMATICO

Hinojo, serpiente y junco.
Aroma, rastro y penumbra.
Aire, tierra y soledad.

(La escala llega a la luna.)

FABULA

Unicornios y cíclopes.

Cuernos de oro
y ojos verdes.

Sobre el acantilado,
en tropel gigantesco,
ilustran el azogue
sin cristal, del mar.

Unicornios y cíclopes.

Una pupila
y una potencia.

¿Quién duda la eficacia
terrible de esos cuernos?

¡Oculta tus blancos,
Naturaleza!

SCHEMATIC NOCTURNE

Fennel, serpent and rush.
Aroma, scent and penumbra.
Air, earth and solitude.

(The ladder reaches to the moon.)

STANLEY READ

FABLE

Unicorns and cyclopses.

Horns of gold
and eyes of green.

Over the steep,
in giant confusion,
they illustrate the unglazed
mercury of the sea.

Unicorns and cyclopses

An eyeball
and a power.

Who doubts the terrible
efficacy of those horns?

Nature!
Conceal your targets!

ROY CAMPBELL

CARACOLA

Me han traído una caracola.

Dentro le canta
un mar de mapa.
Mi corazón
se llena de agua,
con pececillos
de sombra y plata.

Me han traído una caracola.

EL LAGARTO ESTA LLORANDO . . .

El lagarto está llorando.
La lagarta está llorando.

El lagarto y la lagarta
con delantalitos blancos.

Han perdido sin querer
su anillo de desposados.

¡Ay, su anillito de plomo,
ay, su anillito plomado!

Un cielo grande y sin gente
monta en su globo a los pájaros.

El sol, capitán redondo,
lleva un chaleco de raso.

¡Miradlos qué viejos son!
¡Qué viejos son los lagartos!

SNAIL

They have brought me a snail.

Inside it sings
a map-green ocean.
My heart
swells with water,
with small fish
of brown and silver.

They have brought me a snail.

WILLIAM JAY SMITH

THE LIZARD IS CRYING . . .

The he-lizard is crying.
The she-lizard is crying.

The he-lizard and the she-lizard
with little white aprons.

Have lost without wanting to
their wedding ring.

Ah, their little leaden wedding ring,
ah, their little ring of lead!

A large sky without people
carries the birds in its balloon.

The sun, rotund captain,
wears a satin waistcoat.

Look how old they are!
How old the lizards are!

¡Ay, cómo lloran y lloran,
¡ay! ¡ay! cómo están llorando!

CANCION CANTADA

En el gris,
el pájaro Griffón
se vestía de gris.
Y la niña Kikirikí
perdía su blancor
y forma allí.

Para entrar en el gris
me pinté de gris.
¡Y cómo relumbraba
en el gris!

CANCION TONTA

Mamá.
Yo quiero ser de plata.

Hijo,
tendrás mucho frío.

Mamá.
Yo quiero ser de agua.

Hijo,
tendrás mucho frío.

Oh, how they cry and cry,
Oh! Oh! How they go on crying!

STEPHEN SPENDER
AND J. L. GILI

A SONG SUNG

In cold gray
the Griffon bird
was clothed in gray.
And there from little Kikiriki
whiteness and shape
were taken away.

To enter cold gray
I painted myself gray.
And how I sparkled
in the cold gray!

WILLIAM JAY SMITH

SILLY SONG

Mama,
I wish I were silver.

Son,
You'd be very cold.

Mama,
I wish I were water.

Son,
You'd be very cold.

Mamá.
Bórdame en tu almohada.

¡Eso sí!
¡Ahora mismo!

CANCION DE JINETE (1860)

En la luna negra
de los bandoleros,
cantan las espuelas.

Caballito negro.
¿Dónde llevas tu jinete muerto?

. . . Las duras espuelas
del bandido inmóvil
que perdió las riendas.
Caballito frío.
¡Qué perfume de flor de cuchillo!

En la luna negra,
sangraba el costado
de Sierra Morena.

Caballito negro.
¿Dónde llevas tu jinete muerto?

La noche espolea
sus negros ijares
clavándose estrellas.

Caballito frío.
!Qué perfume de flor de cuchillo!

Mama,
Embroider me on your pillow.

That, yes!
Right away!

HARRIET DE ONIS

SONG OF THE RIDER (1860)

In the black moon
of the highwaymen,
the spurs sing.

Little black horse.
Whither with your dead rider?

. . . The hard spurs
of the motionless bandit
who lost his reins.
Little cold horse.
What a scent of the flower of a knife!

In the black moon
bled the mountainside
of Sierra Morena.

Little black horse.
Whither with your dead rider?

The night spurs
its black flanks
piercing with stars.

Little cold horse.
What a scent of the flower of a knife!

En la luna negra,
¡un grito! y el cuerno
largo de la hoguera.

Caballito negro.
¿Dónde llevas tu jinete muerto?

CANCION DE JINETE

Córdoba.
Lejana y sola.

Jaca negra, luna grande,
y aceitunas en mi alforja.
Aunque sepa los caminos
yo nunca llegaré a Córdoba.

Por el llano, por el viento,
jaca negra, luna roja.
La muerte me está mirando
desde las torres de Córdoba.

¡Ay qué camino tan largo!
¡Ay mi jaca valerosa!
¡Ay que la muerte me espera,
antes de llegar a Córdoba!

Córdoba.
Lejana y sola.

In the black moon,
a shriek! and the long
horn of the bonfire.

Little black horse.
Whither with your dead rider?

STEPHEN SPENDER
AND J. L. GILI

RIDER'S SONG

Córdoba.
Far away and alone.

Black pony, big moon,
and olives in my saddle-bag.
Although I know the roads
I'll never reach Córdoba.

Through the plain, through the wind,
black pony, red moon.
Death is looking at me
from the towers of Córdoba.

Ay! How long the road!
Ay! My valiant pony!
Ay! That death should wait me
before I reach Córdoba.

Córdoba.
Far away and alone.

STEPHEN SPENDER
AND J. L. GILI

ES VERDAD

¡Ay qué trabajo me cuesta
quererte como te quiero!

Por tu amor me duele el aire,
el corazón
y el sombrero.

¿Quién me compraría a mí,
este cintillo que tengo
y esta tristeza de hilo
blanco, para hacer pañuelos?

¡Ay qué trabajo me cuesta
quererte como te quiero!

ARBOLE, ARBOLE . . .

Arbolé, arbolé,
seco y verdé.

La niña del bello rostro
está cogiendo aceituna.
El viento, galán de torres,
la prende por la cintura.
Pasaron cuatro jinetes
sobre jacas andaluzas,
con trajes de azul y verde,
con largas capas oscuras.
"Vente a Córdoba, muchacha."
La niña no los escucha.
Pasaron tres torerillos
delgaditos de cintura,
con trajes color naranja

IT IS TRUE

Oh, what an effort it is
to love you as I do!

For love of you, the air,
my heart
and my hat hurt me.

Who will buy of me
this ribbon I have
and this grief of white
linen to make handkerchiefs?

Oh, what an effort it is
to love you as I do!

HARRIET DE ONIS

TREE, TREE . . .

Tree, tree,
dry and green.

The girl of beautiful face
goes gathering olives.
The wind, that suitor of towers,
grasps her round the waist.
Four riders have passed
on Andalusian ponies,
with suits of azure and green,
and long dark cloaks.
"Come to Córdoba, lass."
The girl pays no heed.
Three young bullfighters have passed,
their waists are slender,
their suits orange-coloured,

y espadas de plata antigua.
"Vente a Sevilla, muchacha."
La niña no los escucha.
Cuando la tarde se puso
morada, con luz difusa,
pasó un joven que llevaba
rosas y mirtos de luna.
"Vente a Granada, muchacha."
Y la niña no lo escucha.
La niña del bello rostro
sigue cogiendo aceituna,
con el brazo gris del viento
ceñido por la cintura.
Arbolé, arbolé.
Seco y verdé.

LA LUNA ASOMA

Cuando sale la luna
se pierden las campanas
y aparecen las sendas
impenetrables.

Cuando sale la luna,
el mar cubre la tierra
y el corazón se siente
isla en el infinito.

Nadie come naranjas
bajo la luna llena.
Es preciso comer
fruta verde y helada.

Cuando sale la luna
de cien rostros iguales,

their swords of antique silver.
"Come to Seville, lass."
The girl pays no heed.
When the evening became
purple, with diffused light,
a youth passed by bringing
roses and myrtles of the moon.
"Come to Granada, lass."
But the girl pays no heed.
The girl of beautiful face
still goes on gathering olives,
with the gray arm of the wind
encircling her waist.
Tree, tree.
Dry and green.

STEPHEN SPENDER
AND J. L. GILI

THE MOON RISING

When the moon rises,
the bells hang silent,
and impenetrable footpaths
appear.

When the moon rises,
the sea covers the land,
and the heart feels
like an island in infinity.

Nobody eats oranges
under the full moon.
One must eat fruit
that is green and cold.

When the moon rises,
moon of a hundred equal faces,

la moneda de plata
solloza en el bolsillo.

LA CALLE DE LOS MUDOS

Detrás de las inmóviles vidrieras
las muchachas juegan con sus risas.

    (En los pianos vacíos,
arañas titiriteras.)

Las muchachas hablan con sus novios
agitando sus trenzas apretadas.

    (Mundo del abanico,
el pañuelo y la mano.)

Los galanes replican haciendo
alas y flores con sus capas negras.

MURIO AL AMANECER

Noche de cuatro lunas
y un solo árbol,
con una sola sombra
y un solo pájaro.

Busco en mi carne las
huellas de tus labios.
El manantial besa al viento
sin tocarlo.

the silver coinage
sobs in the pocket.

LYSANDER KEMP

THE STREET OF THE MUTES

Behind the rigid panes
the girls play games with their smiles.

   (Spiders at puppetry
in the empty pianos.)

The girls talk to their suitors,
shaking their tight braids.

   (World of the fan,
the handkerchief and the hand.)

The gallants reply, making
with their black cloaks wings and flowers.

W. S. MERWIN

HE DIED AT DAWN

Night of four moons
and one lone tree,
with one lone shadow
and one lone bird.

I seek in my flesh
the tracks of your lips.
The fountain kisses the wind
without touch.

Llevo el No que me diste,
en la palma de la mano,
como un limón de cera
casi blanco.

Noche de cuatro lunas
y un solo árbol.
En la punta de una aguja,
está mi amor ¡girando!

LA SOLTERA EN MISA

Bajo el Moisés del incienso,
adormecida.

Ojos de toro te miraban.
Tu rosario llovía.

Con ese traje de profunda seda,
no te muevas, Virginia.

Da los negros melones de tus pechos
al rumor de la misa.

EN MALAGA

Suntuosa Leonarda.
Carne pontifical y traje blanco,
en las barandas de "Villa Leonarda".
Expuesta a los tranvias y a los barcos.
Negros torsos bañistas oscurecen
la ribera del mar. Oscilando

I carry the No that you gave me
in the palm of my hand,
like a lemon of wax
almost white.

Night of four moons
and one lone tree.
On a pin's point
my love is spinning!

GREVILLE TEXIDOR

THE SPINSTER AT MASS

Beneath the Moses of the incense,
drowsing.

Bull eyes observe you.
Your rosary raining.

In that dress of silk so dense,
never stir, Virginia.

Give the black melons of your breasts
to the murmur of the mass.

EDWIN HONIG

IN MALAGA

Sumptuous Leonarda.
The flesh pontifical, the garments white,
in the balustrades of Villa Leonarda.
Vulnerable to tramways and to sails.
Black torsos of bathers shadow
the seacoast. And trembling —

—concha y loto a la vez—
viene tu culo
de Ceres en retórica de mármol.

EL NINO MUDO

El niño busca su voz.
(La tenía el rey de los grillos.)
En una gota de agua
buscaba su voz el niño.

No la quiero para hablar;
me haré con ella un anillo
que llevará mi silencio
en su dedo pequeñito.

En una gota de agua
buscaba su voz el niño.

(La voz cautiva, a lo lejos,
se ponía un traje de grillo.)

EL NINO LOCO

Yo decía: "Tarde".
Pero no era así.
La tarde era otra cosa
que ya se había marchado.

(Y la luz encogía
sus hombros como una niña.)

the conch and the lotus together —
the haunches of Ceres
in a rhetoric of marble appear.

BEN BELITT

THE LITTLE MUTE BOY

The little boy was looking for his voice.
(The king of the crickets had it.)
In a drop of water
the little boy was looking for his voice.

I do not want it for speaking with;
I will make a ring of it
so that he may wear my silence
on his little finger.

In a drop of water
the little boy was looking for his voice.

(The captive voice, far away,
put on a cricket's clothes.)

W. S. MERWIN

THE LITTLE MAD BOY

I said: "Afternoon."
But it was not so.
The afternoon was something else
which had already gone away.

(And the light shrugged
its shoulders like a girl.)

ítil!

ѕne

o.

ıunca.

en todos,

jugaba a la ɔ...... con el niño loco.)

Aquella era pequeña
y comía granadas.

Esta es grandota y verde, yo no puedo
tomarla en brazos ni vestirla.
¿No vendrá? ¿Cómo era?

(Y la luz que se iba dió una broma.
Separó al niño loco de su sombra.)

DESPEDIDA

Si muero,
dejad el balcón abierto.

El niño come naranjas.
(Desde mi balcón lo veo.)

El segador siega el trigo.
(Desde mi balcón lo siento.)

¡Si muero,
dejad el balcón abierto!

"Afternoon." But it is useless!
This is false, this has
a half moon made of lead
The other will never come.

(And the light as everyone sees it
played at being a statue, with the mad boy.)

That other: she was little
and ate pomegranates.

This one is huge and green, I cannot
take her in my arms, nor dress her.
Won't she come? What was she like?

(And the light as it went, for a joke,
parted the mad boy from his shadow.)

                    W. S. MERWIN

FAREWELL

If I die,
leave the balcony open.

The little boy is eating oranges.
(From my balcony I can see him.)

The reaper is harvesting the wheat.
(From my balcony I can hear him.)

If I die,
leave the balcony open!

                    W. S. MERWIN

SUICIDIO

*(Quizá fué por no saberte
la geometría.)*

El jovencillo se olvidaba.
Eran las diez de la mañana.

Su corazón se iba llenando
de alas rotas y flores de trapo.

Notó que ya no le quedaba
en la boca más que una palabra.

Y al quitarse los guantes, caía,
de sus manos, suave ceniza.

Por el balcón se veía una torre.
El se sintió balcón y torre.

Vió, sin duda, cómo le miraba
el reloj detenido en su caja.

Vió su sombra tendida y quieta
en el blanco diván de seda.

Y el joven rígido, geométrico,
con un hacha rompió el espejo.

Al romperlo, un gran chorro de sombra,
inundó la quimérica alcoba.

SUICIDE

*(Perhaps because he did
not know his geometry.)*

At ten one morning
the youth forgot.

His heart was growing full
of broken wings and artificial flowers.

He noted in his mouth
but one small word was left.

When he removed his gloves, a fine
thin ash fell from his hands.

From the balcony he saw a tower.
He felt himself both balcony and tower.

Of course he saw how in its frame
the stopped clock observed him.

He saw his shadow stretched out still
upon the silken white divan.

And the boy, rigid, geometric,
broke the mirror with an axe.

When it broke, one huge stream of shadow
flooded his chimeric chamber.

EDWIN HONIG

NARCISO

Narciso.
Tu olor.
Y el fondo del río.

Quiero quedarme a tu vera.
Flor del amor.
Narciso.

Por tus blancos ojos cruzan
ondas y peces dormidos.
Pájaros y mariposas
japonizan en los míos.

Tú diminuto y yo grande.
Flor del amor.
Narciso.

Las ranas ¡qué listas son!
Pero no dejan tranquilo
el espejo en que se miran
tu delirio y mi delirio.

Narciso.
Mi dolor.
Y mi dolor mismo.

DE OTRO MODO

La hoguera pone al campo de la tarde
unas astas de ciervo enfurecido.
Todo el valle se tiende. Por sus lomos,
caracolea el vientecillo.

NARCISSUS

Narcissus.
Your fragrance.
And the depth of the stream.

I would remain at your verge.
Flower of love.
Narcissus.

Over your white eyes flicker
shadows and sleeping fish.
Birds and butterflies
lacquer mine.

You so minute and I so tall.
Flower of love.
Narcissus.

How active the frogs are!
They will not leave alone
the glass which mirrors
your delirium and mine.

Narcissus.
My sorrow.
And my sorrow's self.

                    WILLIAM JAY SMITH

IN ANOTHER MODE

The bonfire places on the field of afternoon
the horns of a maddened deer.
All the valley stretches out. The little wind
is prancing on its ridges.

El aire cristaliza bajo el humo.
—Ojo de gato triste y amarillo—.
Yo, en mis ojos, paseo por las ramas.
Las ramas se pasean por el río.

Llegan mis cosas esenciales.
Son estribillos de estribillos.
Entre los juncos y la baja tarde,
¡qué raro que me llame Federico!

CANCION INUTIL

Rosa futura y vena contenida,
amatista de ayer y brisa de ahora mismo,
        ¡quiero olvidarlas!

Hombre y pez en sus medios, bajo cosas flotantes,
esperando en el alga o en la silla su noche,
        ¡quiero olvidarlas!

                Yo.
            ¡Sólo yo!
        Labrando la bandeja
        donde no irá mi cabeza.
            ¡Sólo yo!

DOS MARINOS EN LA ORILLA

        1
Se trajo en el corazón
un pez del Mar de la China.
A veces se ve cruzar
diminuto por sus ojos.

The air turns crystal under the smoke.
—A cat's eye, sad and yellow—.
I, in my eyes, walk through the boughs.
The boughs walk through the river.

They come to me, my essential things.
They are refrains of refrains.
Here in the reeds in the late afternoon,
how strange to be named Federico!

LYSANDER KEMP

USELESS SONG

Future rose and held vein,
amethyst of yesterday and breeze of this moment,
      I want to forget them!

Man and fish in their medium, under floating things,
waiting, in the algae or in the chair, their night,
      I want to forget them!

I.

I alone!
Hammering the tray
which will not bear my head.
I alone!

W. S. MERWIN

TWO SAILORS ON THE BEACH

1

He wears in his heart
a fish from the China Sea.
At times one sees it crossing,
diminished, in his eyes.

Olvida siendo marino
los bares y las naranjas.

Mira al agua.

2
Tenía la lengua de jabón.
Lavó sus palabras y se calló.

Mundo plano, mar rizado,
cien estrellas y su barco.

Vió los balcones del Papa
y los pechos dorados de las cubanas.

Mira al agua.

ANSIA DE ESTATUA

Rumor.
Aunque no quede más que el rumor.

Aroma.
Aunque no quede más que el aroma.

Pero arranca de mí el recuerdo
y el color de las viejas horas.

Dolor.
Frente al mágico y vivo dolor.

Batalla.
En la auténtica y sucia batalla.

¡Pero quita la gente invisible
que rodea perenne mi casa!

Being seaman he forgets
bars and oranges.

He looks at the water.

2
He had a soapy tongue.
He washed his words and was still.

Level world, hilly sea,
a hundred stars and his ship.

He saw the balconies of the Pope
and the golden breasts of the Cuban girls.

He looks at the water.

DONALD JENKS

DESIRE OF A STATUE

Rumor.
Though nothing may remain but the rumor.

Odor.
Though nothing may remain but the odor.

But tear out of me the memory
and the color of the old hours.

Sorrow.
Facing the magical quick sorrow.

Struggle.
The genuine, the unclean struggle.

But rid me of the invisible people
who forever move about my house!

W. S. MERWIN

CANCION DEL NARANJO SECO

Leñador.
Córtame la sombra.
Líbrame del suplicio
de verme sin toronjas.

¿Por qué nací entre espejos?
El día me da vueltas,
y la noche me copia
en todas sus estrellas.

Quiero vivir sin verme.
Y hormigas y vilanos,
soñaré que son mis
hojas y mis pájaros.

Leñador.
Córtame la sombra.
Líbrame del suplicio
de verme sin toronjas.

SONG OF THE BARREN ORANGE TREE

Woodcutter.
Cut my shadow from me.
Free me from the torment
of seeing myself without fruit.

Why was I born among mirrors?
The day walks in circles around me,
and the night copies me
in all its stars.

I want to live without seeing myself.
And I will dream that ants
and thistleburrs are my
leaves and my birds.

Woodcutter.
Cut my shadow from me.
Free me from the torment
of seeing myself without fruit.

                            W. S. MERWIN

FROM

ROMANCERO GITANO

1924–1927

ROMANCE SONAMBULO

Verde que te quiero verde.
Verde viento. Verdes ramas.
El barco sobre la mar
y el caballo en la montaña.
Con la sombra en la cintura
ella sueña en su baranda,
verde carne, pelo verde,
con ojos de fría plata.
Verde que te quiero verde.
Bajo la luna gitana,
las cosas la están mirando
y ella no puede mirarlas.

Verde que te quiero verde.
Grandes estrellas de escarcha
vienen con el pez de sombra
que abre el camino del alba.
La higuera frota su viento
con la lija de sus ramas,
y el monte, gato garduño,
eriza sus pitas agrias.
¿Pero quién vendra? ¿Y por dónde . . . ?
Ella sigue en su baranda,
verde carne, pelo verde,
soñando en la mar amarga.

—Compadre, quiero cambiar
mi caballo por su casa,
mi montura por su espejo,
mi cuchillo por su manta.
Compadre, vengo sangrando,
desde los puertos de Cabra.
—Si yo pudiera, mocito,
este trato se cerraba.
Pero yo ya no soy yo,
ni mi casa es ya mi casa.

SOMNAMBULE BALLAD

Green, how much I want you green.
Green wind. Green branches.
The ship upon the sea
and the horse in the mountain.
With the shadow on her waist
she dreams on her balcony,
green flesh, hair of green,
and eyes of cold silver.
Green, how much I want you green.
Beneath the gypsy moon,
all things look at her
but she cannot see them.

Green, how much I want you green.
Great stars of white frost
come with the fish of darkness
that opens the road of dawn.
The fig tree rubs the wind
with the sandpaper of its branches,
and the mountain, a filching cat,
bristles its bitter aloes.
But who will come? And from where?
She lingers on her balcony,
green flesh, hair of green,
dreaming of the bitter sea.

—Friend, I want to change
my horse for your house,
my saddle for your mirror,
my knife for your blanket.
Friend, I come bleeding,
from the passes of Cabra.
—If I could, young man,
this pact would be sealed.
But I am no more I,
nor is my house now my house.

—Compadre, quiero morir
decentemente en mi cama.
De acero, si puede ser,
con las sábanas de holanda.
¿No ves la herida que tengo
desde el pecho a la garganta?
—Trescientas rosas morenas
lleva tu pechera blanca.
Tu sangre rezuma y huele
alrededor de tu faja.
Pero yo ya no soy yo,
ni mi casa es ya mi casa.
—Dejadme subir al menos
hasta las altas barandas;
¡dejadme subir!, dejadme,
hasta las verdes barandas.
Barandales de la luna
por donde retumba el agua.

Ya suben los dos compadres
hacia las altas barandas.
Dejando un rastro de sangre.
Dejando un rastro de lágrimas.
Temblaban en los tejados
farolillos de hojalata.
Mil panderos de cristal
herían la madrugada.
Verde que te quiero verde,
verde viento, verdes ramas.
Los dos compadres subieron.
El largo viento dejaba
en la boca un raro gusto
de hiel, de menta y de albahaca.
¡Compadre! ¿Dónde está, díme?
¿Dónde está tu niña amarga?
¡Cuántas veces te esperó!
¡Cuántas veces te esperara,
cara fresca, negro pelo,
en esta verde baranda!

—Friend, I want to die
decently in my bed.
Of iron, if it be possible,
with sheets of fine holland.
Do you not see the wound I have
from my breast to my throat?
—Your white shirt bears
three hundred dark roses.
Your pungent blood oozes
around your sash.
But I am no more I,
nor is my house now my house.
—Let me climb at least
up to the high balustrades:
let me come! Let me come!
up to the green balustrades.
Balustrades of the moon
where the water resounds.

Now the two friends go up
towards the high balustrades.
Leaving a trail of blood,
leaving a trail of tears.
Small lanterns of tin
were trembling on the roofs.
A thousand crystal tambourines
were piercing the dawn.
Green, how much I want you green,
green wind, green branches.
The two friends went up.
The long wind was leaving
in the mouth a strange taste
of gall, mint and sweet-basil.
Friend! Where is she, tell me,
where is your bitter girl?
How often she waited for you!
How often did she wait for you,
cool face, black hair,
on this green balcony!

Sobre el rostro del aljibe
se mecía la gitana.
Verde carne, pelo verde,
con ojos de fría plata.
Un carámbano de luna
la sostiene sobre el agua.
La noche se puso íntima
como una pequeña plaza.
Guardias civiles borrachos
en la puerta golpeaban.
Verde que te quiero verde.
Verde viento. Verdes ramas.
El barco sobre la mar.
Y el caballo en la montaña.

LA CASADA INFIEL

Y que yo me la llevé al río
creyendo que era mozuela,
pero tenía marido.
Fué la noche de Santiago
y casi por compromiso.
Se apagaron los faroles
y se encendieron los grillos.
En las últimas esquinas
toqué sus pechos dormidos,
y se me abrieron de pronto
como ramos de jacintos.
El almidón de su enagua
me sonaba en el oído
como una pieza de seda
rasgada por diez cuchillos.
Sin luz de plata en sus copas
los árboles han crecido,
y un horizonte de perros
ladra muy lejos del río.

Over the face of the cistern
the gypsy girl swayed.
Green flesh, hair of green,
with eyes of cold silver.
An icicle of the moon
suspends her above the water.
The night became as intimate
as a little square.
Drunken civil guards
were knocking at the door.
Green, how much I want you green.
Green wind. Green branches.
The ship upon the sea.
And the horse on the mountain.

STEPHEN SPENDER
AND J. L. GILI

THE FAITHLESS WIFE

So I took her to the river
believing she was a maiden,
but she already had a husband.
It was on Saint James's night
and almost as if I was obliged to.
The lanterns went out
and the crickets lighted up.
In the farthest street corners
I touched her sleeping breasts,
and they opened to me suddenly
like spikes of hyacinth.
The starch of her petticoat
sounded in my ears
like a piece of silk
rent by ten knives.
Without silver light on their foliage
the trees had grown larger
and a horizon of dogs
barked very far from the river.

Pasadas las zarzamoras,
los juncos y los espinos,
bajo su mata de pelo
hice un hoyo sobre el limo.
Yo me quité la corbata.
Ella se quitó el vestido.
Yo el cinturón con revólver.
Ella sus cuatro corpiños.
Ni nardos ni caracolas
tienen el cutis tan fino,
ni los cristales con luna
relumbran con ese brillo.
Sus muslos se me escapaban
como peces sorprendidos,
la mitad llenos de lumbre,
la mitad llenos de frío.
Aquella noche corrí
el mejor de los caminos,
montado en potra de nácar
sin bridas y sin estribos.
No quiero decir, por hombre,
las cosas que ella me dijo.
La luz del entendimiento
me hace ser muy comedido.
Sucia de besos y arena
yo me la llevé del río.
Con el aire se batían
las espadas de los lirios.

Me porté como quien soy.
Como un gitano legítimo.
La regalé un costurero
grande, de raso pajizo,
y no quise enamorarme
porque teniendo marido
me dijo que era mozuela
cuando la llevaba al río.

Past the blackberries,
the reeds and the hawthorn,
underneath her cluster of hair
I made a hollow in the earth.
I took off my tie.
She took off her dress.
I my belt with the revolver.
She her four bodices.
Nor nard nor mother-o'-pearl
have skin so fine,
nor does glass with silver
shine with such brilliance.
Her thighs slipped away from me
like startled fish,
half full of fire,
half full of cold.
That night I ran
on the best of roads
mounted on a nacre mare
without bridle or stirrups.
As a man, I won't repeat
the things she said to me.
The light of understanding
has made me most discreet.
Smeared with sand and kisses
I took her away from the river.
The swords of the lilies
battled with the air.

I behaved like what I am.
Like a proper gypsy.
I gave her a large sewing basket,
of straw-coloured satin,
and I did not fall in love
for although she had a husband
she told me she was a maiden
when I took her to the river.

STEPHEN SPENDER
AND J. L. GILI

SAN RAFAEL (CORDOBA)

I

Coches cerrados llegaban
a las orillas de juncos
donde las ondas alisan
romano torso desnudo.
Coches que el Guadalquivir
tiende en su cristal maduro,
entre láminas de flores
y resonancias de nublos.
Los niños tejen y cantan
el desengaño del mundo,
cerca de los viejos coches
perdidos en el nocturno.
Pero Córdoba no tiembla
bajo el misterio confuso,
pues si la sombra levanta
la arquitectura del humo,
un pie de mármol afirma
su casto fulgor enjuto.
Pétalos de lata débil
recaman los grises puros
de la brisa, desplegada
sobre los arcos de triunfo.
Y mientras el puente sopla
diez rumores de Neptuno,
vendedores de tabaco
huyen por el roto muro.

II

Un solo pez en el agua
que a las dos Córdobas junta:
Blanda Córdoba de juncos.
Córdoba de arquitectura.
Niños de cara impasible
en la orilla se desnudan,

SAINT RAPHAEL (CORDOBA)

I

Closed coaches were coming
to the edge of the rushes
where the waves polish and turn
a Roman torso, naked.
Coaches that Guadalquivir
holds in her glassy ripeness
between the gloss of the flower
and the double depth of the cloud.
Shuttling children sing
the naked truth of the world
around the coaches, old
and lost in the dark of night.
And Córdoba never wavers
in that mysterious dark,
for if the shadow lifts
the structure of its smoke
a marble foot discloses
austere and luminous white,
while petals made of tin
plate the purest grays
of a wind, a breeze unfurled
over triumphal arches;
and while the bridge whispers
ten rumors of King Neptune,
tobacco sellers flee
along the broken wall.

II

One fish alone in the water
that makes two towns of one:
soft Córdoba of rushes,
and Córdoba of stone.
Children with no expression
undress among the rushes,

aprendices de Tobías
y Merlines de cintura,
para fastidiar al pez
en irónica pregunta
si quiere flores de vino
o saltos de media luna.
Pero el pez, que dora el agua
y los mármoles enluta,
les da lección y equilibrio
de solitaria columna.
El Arcángel aljamiado
de lentejuelas oscuras
en el mitin de las ondas
buscaba rumor y cuna.

Un solo pez en el agua.
Dos Córdobas de hermosura.
Córdoba quebrada en chorros.
Celeste Córdoba enjuta.

MUERTE DE ANTONITO EL CAMBORIO

Voces de muerte sonaron
cerca del Guadalquivir.
Voces antiguas que cercan
voz de clavel varonil.
Les clavó sobre las botas
mordiscos de jabalí.
En la lucha daba saltos
jabonados de delfín.
Bañó con sangre enemiga
su corbata carmesí,
pero eran cuatro puñales
y tuvo que sucumbir.
Cuando las estrellas clavan

disciples of Tobias,
slender-waisted Merlins
who plague the single fish
with this ironic riddle,
"Does he want flowers of wine,
or half-moon waterfalls?"
But the fish, who gilds the water
and makes the marble mournful,
gives them a lesson in poise,
a solitary column.
Archangel, a trifle Moorish,
dressed in dark spangles, seeking
where the waves held their meeting
for rumor and for cradle.

One fish alone in the water:
two Córdobas of beauty.
One broken in spurts of water,
one dry in the high heaven.

ROLFE HUMPHRIES

THE DEATH OF ANTONITO EL CAMBORIO

Voices of death resounded
near the Guadalquivir.
Ancient voices which surround
voice of manly carnation.
He nailed through their boots
bites of wild boar.
In the fight he leapt
like the slippery dolphin.
He bathed in enemy blood
his crimson tie,
but there were four daggers
and he could only succumb.
When the stars nail

rejones al agua gris,
cuando los erales sueñan
verónicas de alhelí,
voces de muerte sonaron
cerca del Guadalquivir.

—Antonio Torres Heredia,
Camborio de dura crin,
moreno de verde luna,
voz de clavel varonil:
¿Quién te ha quitado la vida
cerca del Guadalquivir?
—Mis cuatro primos Heredias
hijos de Benamejí.
Lo que en otros no envidiaban,
ya lo envidiaban en mí.
Zapatos color corinto,
medallones de marfil,
y este cutis amasado
con aceituna y jazmín.
— ¡Ay, Antoñito el Camborio,
digno de una Emperatriz!
Acuérdate de la Virgen
porque te vas a morir.
— ¡Ay, Federico García,
llama a la Guardia Civil!
Ya mi talle se ha quebrado
como caña de maíz.

Tres golpes de sangre tuvo,
y se murió de perfil.
Viva moneda que nunca
se volverá a repetir.
Un ángel marchoso pone
su cabeza en un cojín.
Otros de rubor cansado,
encendieron un candil.
Y cuando los cuatro primos

spears on the grey water,
when the yearlings dream
verónicas of gilliflowers,
voices of death resounded
near the Guadalquivir.

—Antonio Torres Heredia,
an authentic Camborio,
dark of green moon,
voice of manly carnation:
Who took your life away
near the Guadalquivir?
—My four cousins the Heredias,
sons of Benamejí.
They did not envy in others
what they envied in me.
Raisin-coloured shoes,
ivory medallions
and this skin kneaded
of olive and jasmine.
—Ah, Antoñito of the Camborios
worthy of an Empress!
Remember the Virgin
because you are to die.
—Ah, Federico Garcia,
call the Guardia Civil!
Already my waist has snapped
like a stalk of maize.

Three gushes of blood,
and he died in profile.
Living coin which never
will be repeated.
A swaggering angel places
his head on a cushion.
Others with a wearied blush
lighted an oil lamp.
And when the four cousins

llegan a Benamejí,
voces de muerte cesaron
cerca del Guadalquivir.

ROMANCE DEL EMPLAZADO

¡Mi soledad sin descanso!
Ojos chicos de mi cuerpo
y grandes de mi caballo,
no se cierran por la noche
ni miran al otro lado
donde se aleja tranquilo
un sueño de trece barcos.
Sino que, limpios y duros
escuderos desvelados,
mis ojos miran un norte
de metales y peñascos
donde mi cuerpo sin venas
consulta naipes helados.

Los densos bueyes del agua
embisten a los muchachos
que se bañan en las lunas
de sus cuernos ondulados.
Y los martillos cantaban
sobre los yunques sonámbulos,
el insomnio del jinete
y el insomnio del caballo.

El veinticinco de junio
le dijeron a el Amargo:
—Ya puedes cortar si gustas
las adelfas de tu patio.
Pinta una cruz en la puerta
y pon tu nombre debajo,

arrive at Benamejí,
voices of death ceased
near the Guadalquivir.

STEPHEN SPENDER
AND J. L. GILI

BALLAD OF ONE DOOMED TO DIE

Loneliness without rest!
The little eyes of my body
and the big eyes of my horse
never close at night
nor look that other way
where quietly disappears
a dream of thirteen boats.
Instead, clean and hard,
squires of wakefulness,
my eyes look for a north
of metals and of cliffs
where my veinless body
consults frozen playing cards.

Heavy water-oxen charge
boys who bathe in the moons
of their rippling horns.
And the hammers sing
 on the somnambulous anvils
the insomnia of the rider
and the insomnia of the horse.

On the twenty-fifth of June
they said to Amargo:
—Now, you may cut, if you wish,
the oleanders in your courtyard.
Paint a cross on your door
and put your name beneath it,

porque cicutas y ortigas
nacerán en tu costado,
y agujas de cal mojada
te morderán los zapatos.
Será de noche, en lo oscuro,
por los montes imantados
donde los bueyes del agua
beben los juncos soñando.
Pide luces y campanas.
Aprende a cruzar las manos
y gusta los aires fríos
de metales y peñascos.
Porque dentro de dos meses
yacerás amortajado.

Espadón de nebulosa
mueve en el aire Santiago.
Grave silencio, de espalda,
manaba el cielo combado.

El veinticinco de junio
abrió sus ojos Amargo,
y el veinticinco de agosto
se tendió para cerrarlos.
Hombres bajaban la calle
para ver al emplazado,
que fijaba sobre el muro
su soledad con descanso.
Y la sábana impecable,
de duro acento romano,
daba equilibrio a la muerte
con las rectas de sus paños.

for hemlock and nettle
shall take root in your side
and needles of wet lime
will bite into your shoes.
It will be night, in the dark,
in the magnetic mountains
where water-oxen drink
in the reeds, dreaming.
Ask for lights and bells.
Learn to cross your hands,
to taste the cold air
of metals and of cliffs
because within two months
you'll lie down shrouded.

Santiago moved his misty
sword in the air.
Dead silence flows over
the shoulder of the curved sky.

On the twenty-fifth of June
Amargo opened his eyes,
and the twenty-fifth of August
he lay down to close them.
Men came down the street
to look upon the doomed one
who cast on the wall his shadow
of loneliness at rest.
And the impeccable sheet
with its hard Roman accent
gave death a certain poise
by the rectitude of its folds.

LANGSTON HUGHES

ROMANCE DE LA GUARDIA CIVIL ESPAÑOLA

Los caballos negros son.
Las herraduras son negras.
Sobre las capas relucen
manchas de tinta y de cera.
Tienen, por eso no lloran,
de plomo las calaveras.
Con el alma de charol
vienen por la carretera.
Jorobados y nocturnos,
por donde animan ordenan
silencios de goma oscura
y miedos de fina arena.
Pasan, si quieren pasar,
y ocultan en la cabeza
una vaga astronomía
de pistolas inconcretas.
¡Oh ciudad de los gitanos!
En las esquinas, banderas.
La luna y la calabaza
con las guindas en conserva.
¡Oh ciudad de los gitanos!
¿Quién te vió y no te recuerda?
Ciudad de dolor y almizcle
con las torres de canela.

Cuando llegaba la noche
noche que noche nochera,
los gitanos en sus fraguas
forjaban soles y flechas.
Un caballo malherido
llamaba a todas las puertas.
Gallos de vidrio cantaban
por Jerez de la Frontera.
El viento vuelve desnudo
la esquina de la sorpresa,
en la noche platinoche,
noche que noche nochera.

BALLAD OF THE SPANISH CIVIL GUARD

Black are the horses.
The horseshoes are black.
On the dark capes glisten
stains of ink and of wax.
Their skulls are leaden,
which is why they don't weep.
With their patent-leather souls
they come down the street.
Hunchbacked and nocturnal,
where they go, they command
silences of dark rubber
and fears like fine sand.
They pass where they want,
and they hide in their skulls
a vague astronomy
of shapeless pistols.
Oh, city of gypsies!
Your corners hung with banners.
The moon and the pumpkin
with mazard berries preserved.
Oh, city of gypsies!
Who could see you and forget?
City of musk and sorrow,
with your cinnamon towers.

And at the fall of night,
the night benighted by nightfall,
the gypsies within their smithies
were forging suns and arrows.
A badly wounded stallion
was knocking at all the doors.
Near Jerez de la Frontera,
loud crowed the cocks of crystal!
Naked, the wind turns
the corner of the surprise
in the silver-dark night
the night benighted by nightfall.

La Virgen y San José
perdieron sus castañuelas,
y buscan a los gitanos
para ver si las encuentran.
La Virgen viene vestida
con un traje de alcaldesa,
de papel de chocolate
con los collares de almendras.
San José mueve los brazos
bajo una capa de seda.
Detrás va Pedro Domecq
con tres sultanes de Persia.
La media luna soñaba
un éxtasis de cigüeña.
Estandartes y faroles
invaden las azoteas.
Por los espejos sollozan
bailarinas sin caderas.
Agua y sombra, sombra y agua
por Jerez de la Frontera.

¡Oh ciudad de los gitanos!
En las esquinas, banderas.
Apaga tus verdes luces
que viene la benemérita.
¡Oh ciudad de los gitanos!
¿Quién te vió y no te recuerda?
Dejadla lejos del mar,
sin peines para sus crenchas.

Avanzan de dos en fondo
a la ciudad de la fiesta.
Un rumor de siemprevivas
invade las cartucheras.
Avanzan de dos en fondo.
Doble nocturno de tela.
El cielo, se les antoja
una vitrina de espuelas.

The Virgin and St. Joseph
have lost their castanets,
and they search for the gypsies
to see if they have found them.
The Virgin comes dressed
in the robe of a Mayoress
made of chocolate paper
with an almond necklace.
St. Joseph moves his arms
under a silken cloak.
And, with three sultans of Persia,
behind marches Pedro Domecq.
The half-moon was dreaming
the ecstasy of a crane.
Standards and street-lamps
invade the flat roofs.
Dancers without hips
are sobbing in the mirrors.
Water and shadow, shadow and water
by Jerez de la Frontera.

Oh, city of gypsies!
Your corners decked with banners.
Put out your green lights,
the Civil Guard is coming!
Oh, city of gypsies!
Who could see you and forget?
(Leave her far from the sea
with no combs for her hairdress.)

They ride in double file
towards the festive streets,
the rustle of everlastings
invades their cartridge belts.
They ride in ranks of two,
a double nocturne in serge.
The sky, so they fancy,
is a show-case of spurs.

La ciudad, libre de miedo,
multiplicaba sus puertas.
Cuarenta guardias civiles
entran a saco por ellas.
Los relojes se pararon,
y el coñac de las botellas
se disfrazó de noviembre
para no infundir sospechas.
Un vuelo de gritos largos
se levantó en las veletas.
Los sables cortan las brisas
que los cascos atropellan.
Por las calles de penumbra
huyen las gitanas viejas
con los caballos dormidos
y las orzas de moneda.
Por las calles empinadas
suben las capas siniestras,
dejando detrás fugaces
remolinos de tijeras.

En el portal de Belén
los gitanos se congregan.
San José, lleno de heridas,
amortaja a una doncella.
Tercos fusiles agudos
por toda la noche suenan.
La Virgen cura a los niños
con salivilla de estrella.
Pero la Guardia Civil
avanza sembrando hogueras,
donde joven y desnuda
la imaginación se quema.
Rosa la de los Camborios,
gime sentada en su puerta
con sus dos pechos cortados
puestos en una bandeja.
Y otras muchachas corrían

The city, free from fear,
multiplied its doors.
Forty Civil Guards
took them by storm.
The clocks ceased to strike
and the bottles of brandy,
to arouse no suspicion,
wore the mask of November.
Among the weathervanes
rose a flight of long screams.
The sabres cut the breeze
that the hooves trampled on.
Along the streets of shadow
old gypsy women run
with their somnolent horses
and their jars full of coins.
And up the steep streets
the sinister capes fleer,
leaving behind them swift
whirlwinds of shears.

The gypsies are all gathered
by the Bethlehem gate.
St. Joseph, full of wounds,
enshrouds a young maid.
Stubborn and sharp, the guns
clatter the whole night through,
while the Virgin is healing children
with drops of star spume.
But the Guardia Civil
comes scattering fires
by which, young and naked,
the imagination is seared.
Rosa of the Camborios
sits moaning by her door.
Her two breasts, cut off,
are lying on a tray.
And other girls flee,

perseguidas por sus trenzas,
en un aire donde estallan
rosas de pólvora negra.
Cuando todos los tejados
eran surcos en la tierra,
el alba meció sus hombros
en largo perfil de piedra.

¡Oh, ciudad de los gitanos!
La Guardia Civil se aleja
por un túnel de silencio
mientras las llamas te cercan.

¡Oh, ciudad de los gitanos!
¿Quién te vió y no te recuerda?
Que te busquen en mi frente.
Juego de luna y arena.

MARTIRIO DE SANTA OLALLA

1. *Panorama de Mérida*

Por la calle brinca y corre
caballo de larga cola,
mientras juegan o dormitan
viejos soldados de Roma.
Medio monte de Minervas
abre sus brazos sin hojas.
Agua en vilo redoraba
las aristas de las rocas.
Noche de torsos yacentes
y estrellas de nariz rota,
aguarda grietas del alba
para derrumbarse toda.
De cuando en cuando sonaban

pursued by their braids,
through the air in which roses
of black powder are bursting.
When all the tile roofs
were but furrows in the soil,
the dawn shrugged her shoulders
in a long stony profile.

Oh, city of gypsies!
The Civil Guard rides away
through a tunnel of silence,
while around you are flames.

Oh, city of gypsies!
Who could see you and forget?
Let them seek you on my brow.
The play of moon and sand.

A. L. LLOYD

THE MARTYRDOM OF SAINT EULALIA

I. *Panorama of Merida*

In the street, a long-tailed horse
is galloping, rearing,
while the old soldiers of Rome
are dicing or sleeping.
Half a mountain of Minervas
opens its leafless arms.
The hanging water is gilding
the ledges of the rocks.
A night of reclining torsos
and of stars with broken muzzles
waits for crevices of dawn
into which it may tumble.
From time to time resound

blasfemias de cresta roja.
Al gemir la santa niña,
quiebra el cristal de las copas.
La rueda afila cuchillos
y garfios de aguda comba:
Brama el toro de los yunques,
y Mérida se corona
de nardos casi despiertos
y tallos de zarzamora.

II. *El Martirio*

Flora desnuda se sube
por escalerillas de agua.
El Cónsul pide bandeja
para los senos de Olalla.
Un chorro de venas verdes
le brota de la garganta.
Su sexo tiembla enredado
como un pájaro en las zarzas.
Por el suelo, ya sin norma,
brincan sus manos cortadas
que aún pueden cruzarse en tenue
oración decapitada.
Por los rojos agujeros
donde sus pechos estaban
se ven cielos diminutos
y arroyos de leche blanca.
Mil arbolillos de sangre
le cubren toda la espalda
y oponen húmedos troncos
al bisturí de las llamas.
Centuriones amarillos
de carne gris, desvelada,
llegan al cielo sonando
sus armaduras de plata.
Y mientras vibra confusa

the red-combed blasphemies.
Moaning, the blessed girl
breaks the crystal of the glasses.
The wheel whets the knives
and the sharp-pointed hooks.
The bull of the anvils bellows,
and Merida is crowned
with brambleberry briars
and the wakening spikenard.

II. *The Martyrðom*

Naked, Flora goes
up the little stairs of water.
For the breasts of Eulalia
the Consul demands a platter.
A jet of green veins
bursts from her throat.
Her sex trembles, disarrayed
like a bird in a thicket.
On the ground, unruly,
her severed hands writhe,
still crossed in a feeble
decapitated prayer.
And through the red holes
where once were her breasts,
tiny skies are now seen
and rivulets of white milk.
A thousand little trees of blood
cover all her back,
and oppose their moist trunks
to the scalpel of the fire.
Yellow centurions, grey-fleshed,
and sleepless in their harness,
reach the sky, clashing
the silver of their armour.
And as a passion of manes and swords

pasión de crines y espadas,
el Cónsul porta en bandeja
senos ahumados de Olalla.

III. *Infierno y gloria*

Nieve ondulada reposa.
Olalla pende del árbol.
Su desnudo de carbón
tizna los aires helados.
Noche tirante reluce.
Olalla muerta en el árbol.
Tinteros de las ciudades
vuelcan la tinta despacio.
Negros maniquíes de sastre
cubren la nieve del campo
en largas filas que gimen
su silencio mutilado.
Nieve partida comienza.
Olalla blanca en el árbol.
Escuadras de níquel juntan
los picos en su costado.

Una Custodia reluce
sobre los cielos quemados,
entre gargantas de arroyo
y ruiseñores en ramos.
¡Saltan vidrios de colores!
Olalla blanca en lo blanco.
Angeles y serafines
dicen: Santo, Santo, Santo.

is shaking in confusion,
the Consul bears on a platter
the smoky breasts of Eulalia.

III. *Hell and Glory*

Here lies the undulating snow.
Eulalia hangs from the tree.
The frozen air is blackened
by her charcoal nudity.
The longdrawn night is glittering.
Eulalia dead upon the tree.
The inkwells of the cities
spill their ink slowly.
Tailors' dummies in black
cover the snow of the fields,
in long files bemoaning
its mutilated silences.
The broken snow is falling.
Eulalia white upon the tree.
In her side, triangles
of nickel are joining their angles.

Across the burnt-out skies
there blazes a monstrance
between throats of rivulets
and branches of nightingales.
Stained-glass springs up!
Eulalia white on a white field.
Angels and seraphim are crying:
Holy, Holy, Holy.

A. L. LLOYD

THAMAR Y AMNON

La luna gira en el cielo
sobre las tierras sin agua
mientras el verano siembra
rumores de tigre y llama.
Por encima de los techos
nervios de metal sonaban.
Aire rizado venía
con los balidos de lana.
La tierra se ofrece llena
de heridas cicatrizadas,
o estremecida de agudos
cauterios de luces blancas.

Thamár estaba soñando
pájaros en su garganta,
al son de panderos fríos
y cítaras enlunadas.
Su desnudo en el alero,
agudo norte de palma,
pido copos a su vientre
y granizo a sus espaldas.
Thamár estaba cantando
desnuda por la terraza.
Alrededor de sus pies,
cinco palomas heladas.
Amnón, delgado y concreto,
en la torre la miraba
llenas las ingles de espuma
y oscilaciones la barba.
Su desnudo iluminado
se tendía en la terraza,
con un rumor entre dientes
de flecha recién clavada.
Amnón estaba mirando
la luna redonda y baja,
y vió en la luna los pechos
durísimos de su hermana.

THAMAR AND AMNON

The moon revolves in the sky
over waterless lands
while summer sows
murmurs of tiger and flame.
Hovering over the roofs
metal nerves are sounding.
Frizzled air rises
from the bleating of wool.
Earth shows itself full
of cicatrized wounds,
or shaken by acute
cauteries of white lights.

Thamar was dreaming,
birds in her throat,
to the sound of cool tambourines
and moon-bathed cithars.
Her nakedness on the eaves,
sharp pole-star of palm,
asks for snow flakes on her belly
and hail on her shoulders.
Thamar was singing
naked on the terrace.
Around her feet,
five frozen pigeons.
Amnon, slender and concrete,
in the tower gazed at her
his loins full of foam
and his beard of vibration.
His illuminated nakedness
was stretched out on the terrace,
with between his teeth a murmur
of newly struck arrow.
Amnon was gazing at
the round and low moon,
and he saw in the moon his sister's
very firm breasts.

Amnón a las tres y media
se tendió sobre la cama.
Toda la alcoba sufría
con sus ojos llenos de alas.
La luz, maciza, sepulta
pueblos en la arena parda,
o descubre transitorio
coral de rosas y dalias.
Linfa de pozo oprimida,
brota silencio en las jarras.
En el musgo de los troncos
la cobra tendida canta.
Amnón gime por la tela
fresquisima de la cama.
Yedra del escalofrío
cubre su carne quemada.
Thamár entró silenciosa
en la alcoba silenciada,
color de vena y Danubio,
turbia de huellas lejanas.
—Thamár, bórrame los ojos
con tu fija madrugada.
Mis hilos de sangre tejen
volantes sobre tu falda.
—Déjame tranquila, hermano.
Son tus besos en mi espalda,
avispas y vientecillos
en doble enjambre de flautas.
—Thamár, en tus pechos altos
hay dos peces que me llaman
y en las yemas de tus dedos
rumor de rosa encerrada.

Los cien caballos del rey
en el patio relinchaban.
Sol en cubos resistía
la delgadez de la parra.
Ya la coge del cabello,

At half-past three Amnon
stretched himself on his bed.
The whole alcove suffered
with his eyes full of wings.
The thick light buries
villages in the brown sand,
or discovers momentary
coral of roses and dahlias.
Water from the well, oppressed,
blossoms silence in the jars.
On the moss of tree trunks
the stretched cobra sings.
Amnon groans between the cold
sheets of his bed.
The ivy of shivering
spreads over his parched flesh.
Thamar entered silent
in the silenced alcove,
colour of vein and Danube
troubled with remote trails.
—Thamar, efface these eyes
with your steadfast dawn.
My threads of blood weave
flounces over your skirt.
—Leave me in peace, brother.
Your kisses in my shoulder
are wasps and light breezes
in a double swarm of flutes.
—Thamar, in your turgent breasts
are two fishes calling me,
and in the tips of your fingers
are murmurs of sealed rose.

The hundred horses of the king
neighed in the courtyard.
The slenderness of the vine
resisted the sun in squares.
Now he grasps her by the hair,

ya la camisa le rasga.
Corales tibios dibujan
arroyos en rubio mapa.

¡Oh, qué gritos se sentían
por encima de las casas!
Qué espesuras de puñales
y túnicas desgarradas.
Por las escaleras tristes
esclavos suben y bajan.
Embolos y muslos juegan
bajo las nubes paradas.
Alrededor de Thamár
gritan vírgenes gitanas
y otras recogen tas gotas
de su flor martirizada.
Paños blancos enrojecen
en las alcobas cerradas.
Rumores de tibia aurora
pámpanos y peces cambian.

Violador enfurecido,
Amnón huye con su jaca.
Negros le dirigen flechas
en los muros y atalayas.
Y cuando los cuatro cascos
eran cuatro resonancias,
David con unas tijeras
cortó las cuerdas del arpa.

now he claws her dress.
Tepid corals draw
rivulets on a golden map.

Oh, what screams were heard
above the houses!
What thickness of daggers
and ripped-up tunics.
Along the sad stairways
slaves go up and down.
Pistons and thighs play
under suspended clouds.
Around Thamar
gypsy virgins scream
and others collect the drops
of her martyrized flower.
White fabrics redden
in the closed alcoves.
Rumours of cool aurora
vine-tendrils and fishes change.

Amnon, enraged violator,
flees away on his pony.
Negroes aim arrows at him
from ramparts and towers.
And when the four hoofs
were just four echoes,
David, with a pair of scissors,
cut the strings of his harp.

STEPHEN SPENDER
AND J. L. GILI

FROM

POETA EN NUEVA YORK

1929–1930

FABULA Y RUEDA DE LOS TRES AMIGOS

Enrique,
Emilio,
Lorenzo,
Estaban los tres helados:
Enrique por el mundo de las camas;
Emilio por el mundo de los ojos y las heridas de las manos,
Lorenzo por el mundo de las universidades sin tejados.

Lorenzo,
Emilio,
Enrique,
Estaban los tres quemados:
Lorenzo por el mundo de las hojas y las bolas de billar;
Emilio por el mundo de la sangre y los alfileres blancos,
Enrique por el mundo de los muertos y los periódicos
      abandonados.

Lorenzo,
Emilio,
Enrique,
Estaban los tres enterrados:
Lorenzo en un seno de Flora;
Emilio en la yerta ginebra que se olvida en el vaso,
Enrique en la hormiga, en el mar y en los ojos vacíos de los pájaros.

Lorenzo,
Emilio,
Enrique,
Fueron los tres en mis manos
tres montañas chinas,
tres sombras de caballo,
tres paisajes de nieve y una cabaña de azucenas
por los palomares donde la luna se pone plana bajo el gallo.

FABLE AND ROUND OF THE THREE FRIENDS

Enrique,
Emilio,
Lorenzo,
frozen, the three of them:
Enrique in the world of the bed,
Emilio in the world of the eye and the hand's laceration,
Lorenzo in the world of the roofless academies.

Lorenzo,
Emilio,
Enrique,
burning, the three of them:
Lorenzo in the world of the leaves and the cue balls,
Emilio in the world of the blood and white pins,
Enrique in the world of the dead and the castaway tabloids.

Lorenzo,
Emilio,
Enrique,
buried, the three of them:
Lorenzo in a breast of Flora;
Emilio in the still gin, in the wine-glass, forgotten;
Enrique, in the ant, in the sea, in the vacuous eyes of the birds.

Lorenzo,
Emilio,
Enrique,
held in my hands, the three of them,
three Chinese mountains,
three horses' shadows,
three snowy perspectives and a cabin of lilies
among dovecotes where the moon lay outstretched for the rooster.

Uno

y uno
y uno,
Estaban los tres momificados,
con las moscas del invierno,
con los tinteros que orina el perro y desprecia el vilano,
con la brisa que hiela el corazón de todas las madres,
por los blancos derribos de Júpiter donde meriendan muerte
     los borrachos.

Tres

y dos
y uno,
Los vi perderse llorando y cantando
por un huevo de gallina,
por la noche que enseñaba su esqueleto de tabaco,
por mi dolor lleno de rostros y punzantes esquirlas de luna,
por mi alegría de ruedas dentadas y látigos,
por mi pecho turbado por las palomas,
por mi muerte desierta con un solo paseante equivocado.

Yo había matado la quinta luna
y bebían agua por las fuentes los abanicos y los aplausos.
Tibia leche encerrada de las recién paridas
agitaba las rosas con un largo dolor blanco,
Enrique,
Emilio,
Lorenzo.
Diana es dura,
pero a veces tiene los pechos nublados.
Puede la piedra blanca latir en la sangre del ciervo
y el ciervo puede soñar por los ojos de un caballo.

Cuando se hundieron las formas puras
bajo el cri cri de las margaritas,

110

One

and one
and one,
mummied, the three of them,
with the houseflies of winter,
with inkwells fouled by the dogs, and scorned by the cockle-burr,
with the wind that freezes the hearts of all mothers,
through the white demolitions of Jupiter where the drunkards nibble
    on death.

Three

and two
and one,
I saw them despoil themselves, sobbing and singing,
for a hen's egg,
for a night that displayed its tobacco-leaf skeleton,
for my woe full of faces and piercing moon splinters,
for my joy in the tooth of the wheel and the lash of the whip,
for my breast shaken with doves,
for my derelict dying, with a single mistaken bypasser.

I had killed the fifth moon
and the fans and the handclapping drank at the fountains.
The milk of the newly delivered, still tepid and sealed,
troubled the roses with its long white grief.
Enrique,
Emilio,
Lorenzo.
Diana is hard,
but sometimes her bosom goes cloudy.
Even the white stone may pulse in the blood of a stag
and the stag have its dream in the eyes of a stallion.

When the pure forms collapsed
in the *cri-cri* of daisies,

comprendí que me habían asesinado.
Recorrieron los cafés y los cementerios y las iglesias,
abrieron los toneles y los armarios,
destrozaron tres esqueletos para arrancar sus dientes de oro.
Ya no me encontraron.
¿No me encontraron?
No. No me encontraron.
Pero se supo que la sexta luna huyó torrente arriba,
y que el mar recordó ¡de pronto!
los nombres de todos sus ahogados.

TU INFANCIA EN MENTON

Sí, tu niñez ya fábula de fuentes.

JORGE GUILLÉN

Sí, tu niñez ya fábula de fuentes.
El tren y la mujer que llena el cielo.
Tu soledad esquiva en los hoteles
y tu máscara pura de otro signo.
Es la niñez del mar y tu silencio
donde los sabios vidrios se quebraban.
Es tu yerta ignorancia donde estuvo
mi torso limitado por el fuego.
Norma de amor te di, hombre de Apolo,
llanto con ruiseñor enajenado,
pero, pasto de ruina, te afilabas
para los breves sueños indecisos.
Pensamiento de enfrente, luz de ayer,
índices y señales del acaso.
Tu cintura de arena sin sosiego
atiende sólo rastros que no escalan.
Pero yo he de buscar por los rincones
tu alma tibia sin ti que no te entiende,
con el dolor de Apolo detenido
con que he roto la máscara que llevas.

it came to me that they had murdered me.
They ransacked the cafés, the graveyards, the churches,
they opened the wine-casks and wardrobes,
they ravaged three skeletons to gouge out the gold of their teeth.
But me, they never encountered.
They never encountered me?
No. Never encountered me.
Still, it was known that the sixth moon fled up the torrent,
and the sea could remember — suddenly! —
the names of all its drowned.

BEN BELITT

YOUR CHILDHOOD IN MENTON

*"Yes, your childhood now
a legend of fountains."*
JORGE GUILLÉN

Yes, your childhood now a legend of fountains.
The train, and the woman who fills the sky.
Your evasive solitude in hotels
and your pure mask of another sign.
It is the sea's childhood and the silence
where wisdom's glasses all are shattered.
It is your inert ignorance of where
my torso lay, bound by fire.
Man of Apollo, I gave you love's pattern,
the frenzied nightingale's lament.
But, pasture of ruins, you kept lean
for brief and indecisive dreams.
Thought of what was confronted, yesterday's light,
tokens and traces of chance.
Your restless waist of sand
favors only tracks that don't ascend.
But I must search all corners
for your tepid soul without you which doesn't understand you
with my thwarted Apollonian sorrow
that broke through the mask you wear.

Allí, león, allí, furia del cielo,
te dejaré pacer en mis mejillas;
allí, caballo azul de mi locura,
pulso de nebulosa y minutero,
he de buscar las piedras de alacranes
y los vestidos de tu madre niña,
llanto de media noche y paño roto
que quitó luna de la sien del muerto.
Sí, tu niñez ya fábula de fuentes.
Alma extraña de mi hueco de venas,
te he de buscar pequeña y sin raíces.
¡Amor de siempre, amor, amor de nunca!
¡Oh, sí! Yo quiero. ¡Amor, amor! Dejadme.
No me tapen la boca los que buscan
espigas de Saturno por la nieve
o castran animales por un cielo,
clínica y selva de la anatomía.
Amor, amor, amor. Niñez del mar.
Tu alma tibia, sin ti que no te entiende.
Amor, amor, un vuelo de la corza
por el pecho sin fin de la blancura.
Y tu niñez, amor, y tu niñez.
El tren y la mujer que llena el cielo.
Ni tú, ni yo, ni el aire, ni las hojas.
Si, tu niñez ya fábula de fuentes.

EL REY DE HARLEM

Con una cuchara
arrancaba los ojos a los cocodrilos
y golpeaba el trasero de los monos.
Con una cuchara.

Fuego de siempre dormía en los pedernales
y los escarabajos borrachos de anís
olvidaban el musgo de las aldeas.

There, lion, there, heavenly fury,
I'll let you graze on my cheeks;
there, blue horse of my madness,
pulse of nebula and minute hand,
I'll search the stones for scorpions
and your childlike mother's clothes,
midnight lament and ragged cloth
that tore the moon out of the dead man's brow.
Yes, your childhood now a legend of fountains.
Soul a stranger to my veins' emptiness,
I'll search for you rootless and small.
Eternal love, love, love that never was!
Oh, yes! I love. Love, love! Leave me.
Don't let them gag me, they who seek
the wheat of Saturn through the snow,
who castrate creatures in the sky,
clinic and wilderness of anatomy.
Love, love, love. Childhood of the sea.
Your tepid soul without you which doesn't understand you.
Love, love, a flight of deer
through the endless heart of whiteness.
And your childhood, love, your childhood.
The train, and the woman who fills the sky.
Not you or I, not the wind or the leaves.
Yes, your childhood now a legend of fountains.

EDWIN HONIG

THE KING OF HARLEM

With a spoon
he scooped out the eyes of crocodiles
and spanked the monkeys on their bottoms.
With a spoon.

Fire of all times slept in the flints
and the beetles drunk with anis
forgot the moss of the villages.

Aquel viejo cubierto de setas
iba al sitio donde lloraban los negros
mientras crujía la cuchara del rey
y llegaban los tanques de agua podrida.

Las rosas huían por los filos
de las últimas curvas del aire,
y en los montones de azafrán
los niños machacaban pequeñas ardillas
con un rubor de frenesí manchado.

Es preciso cruzar los puentes
y llegar al rubor negro
para que el perfume de pulmón
nos golpee las sienes con su vestido
de caliente piña.

Es preciso matar al rubio vendedor de aguardiente,
a todos los amigos de la manzana y de la arena,
y es necesario dar con los puños cerrados
a las pequeñas judías que tiemblan llenas de burbujas,
para que el rey de Harlem cante con su muchedumbre,
para que los cocodrilos duerman en largas filas
bajo el amianto de la luna,
y para que nadie dude de la infinita belleza
de los plumeros, los ralladores, los cobres y las cacerolas de las cocinas.

¡ Ay, Harlem! ¡ Ay, Harlem! ¡ Ay, Harlem!
No hay angustia comparable a tus rojos oprimidos,
a tu sangre estremecida dentro del eclípse oscuro,
a tu violencia granate sordomuda en la penumbra,
a tu gran rey prisionero, con un traje de conserje.

Tenía la noche una hendidura y quietas salamandras de marfil.
Las muchachas americanas
llevaban niños y monedas en el vientre
y los muchachos se desmayaban en la cruz del desperezo.

That old man covered with mushrooms
went to the place where the Negroes were weeping
while the spoon of the King crackled
and the tanks of putrid water arrived.

Roses escaped along the edge of the final curves of the air,
and in the heaps of saffron
the boys were mauling small squirrels
with a flush of stained frenzy.

It is necessary to cross the bridges
and to reach the black murmur,
so that the perfume of lungs strikes our temples
with its suit of warm pineapple.

Necessary to murder the blonde seller of brandy,
and all the friends of the apple and sand,
necessary to bang with closed fists
the small Jewesses that tremble full of bubbles,
so that the King of Harlem sings with his multitude,
so that the crocodiles sleep in long rows
under the asbestos of the moon,
so that nobody doubts the infinite beauty of funnels,
graters, feather-dusters, and saucepans in kitchens.

Ah Harlem! Ah Harlem! Ah Harlem!
There is no anxiety comparable to your oppressed scarlets,
to your blood shaken within your dark eclipse,
to your garnet violence deaf and dumb in the penumbra,
to your great King, a prisoner with a commissionaire's uniform.

The night had a fissure
and still ivory salamanders.
The American girls carried babies and coins in their bellies
and the boys fainted stretched on the cross of lassitude.

Ellos son.
Ellos son los que beben el whisky de plata junto a los volcanes
y tragan pedacitos de corazón por las heladas montañas del oso.

Aquella noche el rey de Harlem con una durísima cuchara
arrancaba los ojos a los cocodrilos
y golpeaba el trasero de los monos.
Con una cuchara.
Los negros lloraban confundidos
entre paraguas y soles de oro,
los mulatos estiraban gomas, ansiosos de llegar al torso blanco,
y el viento empañaba espejos
y quebraba las venas de los bailarines.

   Negros, Negros, Negros, Negros.

La sangre no tiene puertas en vuestra noche boca arriba.
No hay rubor. Sangre furiosa por debajo de las pieles, ·
viva en la espina del puñal y en el pecho de los paisajes,
bajo las pinzas y las retamas de la celeste luna de cáncer.

Sangre que busca por mil caminos muertes enharinadas y ceniza
      de nardo,
cielos yertos, en declive, donde las colonias de planetas
rueden por las playas con los objetos abandonados.

Sangre que mira lenta con el rabo del ojo,
hecha de espartos exprimidos, néctares de subterráneos.
Sangre que oxida el alisio descuidado en una huella
y disuelve a las mariposas en los cristales de la ventana.

Es la sangre que viene, que vendrá
por los tejados y azoteas, por todas partes,
para quemar la clorofila de las mujeres rubias,
para gemir al pie de las camas ante el insomnio de los lavabos
y estrellarse en una aurora de tabaco y bajo amarillo.

Hay que huir,
huir por las esquinas y encerrarse en los últimos pisos,

They are.
They are those who take silver whisky near the volcanoes
and devour bits of heart through the frozen mountains of the bear.

That night the King of Harlem with a very hard spoon
scooped out the eyes of crocodiles
and spanked the monkeys on their bottoms.
With a spoon.
The Negroes cried abased
among umbrellas and golden suns,
the mulattoes were stretching gum, anxious to reach the white torso,
and the wind blurred mirrors
and burst open the veins of the dancers.

   Negroes, Negroes, Negroes, Negroes.

The blood has no doors in your night face upwards.
There is no blushing. Furious blood under the skins,
alive in the thorn of the dagger and in the breast of landscapes,
under the pincers and the broom of the celestial Moon of Cancer.

Blood that searches through thousand ways deaths covered in flour
       and ashes of nards,
still skies, slanting, where the colonies of planets
tumble along beaches with abandoned objects.

Blood that looks slowly through the tail of the eye
made of squeezed esparto and subterranean nectars.
Blood that oxidizes the unaware trade wind in a footprint
and dissolves the butterflies in the windowpanes.

This is the blood that comes, that will come
through roofs and terraces, by every way,
to burn the chlorophyll of blonde women,
to groan at the foot of beds facing insomnia of basins
and to crash against a dawn of tobacco and subdued yellow.

One has to flee,
to flee from the shores and lock oneself up in the top storeys

porque el tuétano del bosque penetrará por las rendijas
para dejar en vuestra carne una leve huella de eclipse
y una falsa tristeza de guante desteñido y rosa química.

Es por el silencio sapientísimo
cuando los camareros y los cocineros y los que limpian con la lengua
las heridas de los millonarios
buscan al rey por las calles o en los ángulos del salitre.

Un viento sur de madera, oblicuo en el negro fango,
escupe a las barcas rotas y se clava puntillas en los hombros;
un viento sur que lleva
colmillos, girasoles, alfabetos
y una pila de Volta con avispas ahogadas.

El olvido estaba expresado por tres gotas de tinta sobre el monóculo,
el amor por un solo rostro invisible a flor de piedra.
Médulas y corolas componían sobre las nubes
un desierto de tallos sin una sola rosa.

A la izquierda, a la derecha, por el sur y por el norte,
se levanta el muro impasible
para el topo, la aguja del agua.
No busquéis, negros, su grieta
para hallar la máscara infinita.
Buscad el gran sol del centro
hechos una piña zumbadora.
El sol que se desliza por los bosques
seguro de no encontrar una ninfa,
el sol que destruye números y no ha cruzado nunca un sueño,
el tatuado sol que baja por el río
y muge seguido de caimanes.

   Negros, Negros, Negros, Negros.

Jamás sierpe, ni cebra, ni mula
palidecieron al morir.
El leñador no sabe cuándo expiran

because the marrow of the woods will penetrate through the crevices,
to leave in your flesh a slight print of eclipse
and a false sadness of faded glove and chemical rose.

Through the most wise silence
when the waiters and cooks and those that clean with their tongues
the wounds of millionaires
look for the King through the streets and in angles of saltpeter.

An oblique South Wind of wood in the black mud
spits at the broken boats and pierces nails in its shoulders;
a South Wind that carries
fangs, sunflowers, alphabets
and a voltaic battery with suffocated wasps.

Oblivion was expressed by three drops of ink on the monocle,
love, by a single face, invisible on the surface of stone.
Marrows and corollas were composing on the clouds
a desert of stems without a single rose.

From the left, from the right, from the South, and from the North,
there rises the wall impassive
to the mole and the needle of water.
Do not seek, Negroes, for the cleft
to find the infinite mask.
Seek for the great Sun of the center
made into a buzzing cluster.
The Sun that slides through the woods
certain of not meeting a nymph,
the Sun that destroys numbers and has never crossed a dream,
the tattooed Sun that goes down the river
and bellows followed by alligators.

Negroes, Negroes, Negroes, Negroes.

Never snake, nor goat, nor mule
grew pale at death.
The wood-cutter does not know when

los clamorosos árboles que corta.
Aguardad bajo la sombra vegetal de vuestro rey
a que cicutas y cardos y ortigas turben postreras azoteas.

Entonces, negros, entonces, entonces,
podréis besar con frenesí las ruedas de las bicicletas,
poner parajas de microscopios en las cuevas de las ardillas
y danzar al fin, sin duda, mientras las flores erizadas
asesinan a nuestro Moisés casi en los juncos del cielo.

¡Ay, Harlem, disfrazada!
¡Ay, Harlem, amenazada por un gentío de trajes sin cabeza!
Me llega tu rumor,
me llega tu rumor atravesando troncos y ascensores,
a través de láminas grises
donde flotan tus automóviles cubiertos de dientes,
a través de los caballos muertos y los crímenes diminutos,
a través de tu gran rey desesperado
cuyas barbas llegan al mar.

LA AURORA

La Aurora de Nueva York tiene
cuatro columnas de cieno
y un huracán de negras palomas
que chapotean las aguas podridas.

La aurora de Nueva York gime
por las inmensas escaleras
buscando entre las aristas
nardos de angustia dibujada.

La aurora llega y nadie la recibe en su boca
porque allí no hay mañana ni esperanza posible.

the clamorous trees which he fells expire.
Wait under the vegetable shadow of your King
until the hemlock, thistles and stinging nettles disturb the
        furthermost terraces.

Then, Negroes, then, then,
you will be able to kiss with frenzy the wheels of bicycles,
to put pairs of microscopes in the caves of the squirrels
and dance at last, without fear, while the spiked flowers
assassinate our Moses almost in the reeds of Heaven!

Ah, masqueraded Harlem!
Ah, Harlem, threatened by a mob wearing clothes without heads!
Your rumour reaches me,
your rumour reaches me, crossing tree trunks and lifts,
across the grey plates
where your cars float covered with teeth,
across the dead horses and the minute crimes,
across your great despairing King,
whose beard reaches the sea.

STEPHEN SPENDER
AND J. L. GILI

THE DAWN

The New York dawn has
four columns of mud
and a hurricane of black doves
that paddle in putrescent waters.

The New York dawn grieves
along the immense stairways,
seeking amidst the groins
spikenards of fine-drawn anguish.

The dawn comes and no one receives it in his mouth,
for there no morn or hope is possible.

A veces las monedas en enjambres furiosos
taladran y devoran abandonados niños.

Los primeros que salen comprenden con sus huesos
que no habrá paraíso ni amores deshojados;
saben que van al cieno de números y leyes,
a los juegos sin arte, a sudores sin fruto.

La luz es sepultada por cadenas y ruidos
en impúdico reto de ciencia sin raíces.
Por los barrios hay gentes que vacilan insomnes
como recién salidas de un naufragio de sangre.

ODA A WALT WHITMAN

Por el East River y el Bronx,
los muchachos cantaban enseñando sus cinturas,
con la rueda, el aceite, el cuero y el martillo.
Noventa mil mineros sacaban la plata de las rocas
y los niños dibujaban escaleras y perspectivas.

Pero ninguno se dormía,
ninguno quería ser el río,
ninguno amaba las hojas grandes,
ninguno la lengua azul de la playa.

Por el East River y el Queensborough
los muchachos luchaban con la industria
y los judíos vendían al fauno del río
la rosa de la circuncisión
y el cielo desembocaba por los puentes y los tejados
manadas de bisontes empujadas por el viento.

Pero ninguno se detenía,
ninguno quería ser nube,

Occasionally, coins in furious swarms
perforate and devour abandoned children.

The first to come out understand in their bones
that there will be no paradise nor amours stripped of leaves:
they know they are going to the mud of figures and laws,
to artless games, to fruitless sweat.

The light is buried under chains and noises
in impudent challenge of rootless science.
Through the suburbs sleepless people stagger,
as though just delivered from a shipwreck of blood.

STEPHEN SPENDER
AND J. L. GILI

ODE TO WALT WHITMAN

Along the East River and the Bronx
the boys were singing showing their waists,
with the wheel, the oil, the leather and the hammer.
Ninety thousand miners extracted silver from rocks
and children drew stairs and perspectives.

But none would sleep,
none wanted to be a river,
none loved the great leaves,
none, the blue tongue of the beach.

Along the East River and the Queensborough
the boys were fighting with Industry,
and the Jews were selling to the faun of the river
the rose of the Circumcision,
and the sky rushed through bridges and roofs
herds of bison pushed by the wind.

But none would pause,
none wanted to be a cloud,

ninguno buscaba los helechos
ni la rueda amarilla del tamboril.

Cuando la luna salga
las poleas rodarán para turbar el cielo;
un límite de agujas cercará la memoria
y los ataúdes se llevarán a los que no trabajan.

Nueva York de cieno,
Nueva York de alambres y de muerte.
¿Qué angel llevas oculto en la mejilla?
¿Qué voz perfecta dirá las verdades del trigo?
¿Quién el sueño terrible de tus anémonas manchadas?

Ni un solo momento, viejo hermoso Walt Whitman,
he dejado de ver tu barba llena de mariposas,
ni tus hombros de pana gastados por la luna,
ni tus muslos de Apolo virginal,
ni tu voz como una columna de ceniza;
anciano hermoso como la niebla
que gemías igual que un pájaro
con el sexo atravesado por una aguja,
enemigo del sátiro,
enemigo de la vid
y amante de los cuerpos bajo la burda tela.
Ni un solo momento, hermosura viril
que en montes de carbón, anuncios y ferrocarriles,
soñabas ser un río y dormir como un río
con aquel camarada que pondría en tu pecho
un pequeño dolor de ignorante leopardo.

Ni un solo momento, Adán de sangre, macho,
hombre solo en el mar, viejo hermoso Walt Whitman,
porque por las azoteas,
agrupados en los bares,
saliendo en racimos de las alcantarillas,
temblando entre las piernas de los chauffeurs
o girando en las plataformas del ajenjo,
los maricas, Walt Whitman, te señalan.

none searched for the ferns
nor the yellow wheel of the tambourine.

When the moon rises,
the pulleys will turn to disturb the sky:
a boundary of needles will fence in the memory
and the coffins will carry away those who do not work.

New York of slime,
New York of wires and death:
What angel do you carry hidden in your cheek?
What perfect voice will tell the truths of the wheat?
Who, the terrible dream of your stained anemones?

Not for one moment, beautiful aged Walt Whitman,
have I failed to see your beard full of butterflies,
nor your shoulders of corduroy worn out by the moon,
nor your thighs of virginal Apollo,
nor your voice like a pillar of ashes:
ancient and beautiful as the mist,
you moaned like a bird
with the sex transfixed by a needle,
enemy of the satyr,
enemy of the vine,
and lover of bodies under the rough cloth.
Not for one moment; virile beauty,
who in mountains of coal, posters and railways,
dreamed of being a river and sleeping like a river
with that comrade who would place in your breast
the small pain of an ignorant leopard.

Not for one moment, Adam of blood, male,
lone man in the sea, beautiful aged Walt Whitman,
because through the terraces,
clustered around the bars,
pouring out of sewers in bunches,
trembling between the legs of chauffeurs
or revolving on the platforms of absinthe,
the pansies, Walt Whitman, dreamed of you.

¡También ése! ¡También! Y se despeñan
sobre tu barba luminosa y casta,
rubios del norte, negros de la arena,
muchedumbres de gritos y ademanes,
como gatos y como las serpientes,
los maricas, Walt Whitman, los maricas
turbios de lágrimas, carne para fusta,
bota o mordisco de los domadores.

¡También ése! ¡También! Dedos teñidos
apuntan a la orilla de tu sueño
cuando el amigo come tu manzana
con un leve sabor de gasolina
y el sol canta por los ombligos
de los muchachos que juegan bajo los puentes.

Pero tú no buscabas los ojos arañados,
ni el pantano oscurísimo donde sumergen a los niños,
ni la saliva helada,
ni las curvas heridas como panza de sapo
que llevan los maricas en coches y terrazas
mientras la luna los azota por las esquinas del terror.

Tú buscabas un desnudo que fuera como un río,
toro y sueño que junte la rueda con el alga,
padre de tu agonía, camelia de tu muerte,
y gimiera en las llamas de tu ecuador oculto.

Porque es justo que el hombre no busque su deleite
en la selva de sangre de la mañana próxima.
El cielo tiene playas donde evitar la vida
y hay cuerpos que no deben repetirse en la aurora.

Agonía, agonía, sueño, fermento y sueño.
Este es el mundo, amigo, agonía, agonía.
Los muertos se descomponen bajo el reloj de las ciudades,
la guerra pasa llorando con un millón de ratas grises,
los ricos dan a sus queridas

This one also! This one! And they fall
on your chaste and luminous beard,
Northern blonds, Negroes of the sands,
multitudes of shrieks and gestures,
like cats or like snakes,
the pansies, Walt Whitman, the pansies,
muddy with tears, flesh for the whip,
boot or bite of subduers.

This one also! This one! Tainted fingers
appear on the shore of your dreams
when the friend eats your apple
with a faint taste of petrol
and the sun sings along the navels
of boys that play under bridges.

But you did not search for the scratched eyes,
or the very dark swamp where children are submerged,
or the frozen saliva,
or the wounded curves resembling toad's bellies
which the pansies carry in cars and terraces
while the moon strikes at them along the corners of fear.

You searched for a nude who was like a river.
Bull and dream that would join the wheel with the seaweed,
father of your agony, camellia of your death,
and would moan in the flames of your hidden Equator.

Because it is just that man does not search for his delight
in the jungle of blood of the following morning.
The sky has shores where to avoid life,
and certain bodies must not repeat themselves in the dawn.

Agony, agony, dream, ferment and dream.
This is the world, my friend, agony, agony.
The corpses decompose under the clock of the cities.
War passes weeping with a million grey rats,
the rich give to their mistresses

pequeños moribundos iluminados,
y la vida no es noble, ni buena, ni sagrada.

Puede el hombre, si quiere, conducir su deseo
por vena de coral o celeste desnudo.
Mañana los amores serán rocas y el Tiempo
una brisa que viene dormida por las ramas.

Por eso no levanto mi voz, viejo Walt Whitman,
contra el niño que escribe
nombre de niña en su almohada,
ni contra el muchacho que se viste de novia
en la oscuridad del ropero,
ni contra los solitarios de los casinos
que beben con asco el agua de la prostitución,
ni contra los hombres de mirada verde
que aman al hombre y queman sus labios en silencio.
Pero sí contra vosotros, maricas de las ciudades,
de carne tumefacta y pensamiento inmundo,
madres de lodo, arpías, enemigos sin sueño
del Amor que reparte coronas de alegría.

Contra vosotros siempre, que dais a los muchachos
gotas de sucia muerte con amargo veneno.
Contra vosotros siempre,
Faeries de Norteamérica,
Pájaros de la Habana,
Jotos de Méjico,
Sarasas de Cádiz,
Apios de Sevilla,
Cancos de Madrid,
Floras de Alicante,
Adelaidas de Portugal.

¡Maricas de todo el mundo, asesinos de palomas!
Esclavos de la mujer, perras de sus tocadores,
abiertos en las plazas con fiebre de abanico
o emboscadas en yertos paisajes de cicuta.

small illuminated moribunds,
and Life is not noble, nor good, nor sacred.

Man can, if he wishes, lead his desire
through vein of coral or celestial nude:
tomorrow love will be rocks, and Time
a breeze which comes sleeping through the branches.

That is why I do not raise my voice, aged Walt Whitman,
against the little boy who writes
a girl's name on his pillow,
nor the boy who dresses himself in the bride's trousseau
in the darkness of the wardrobe,
nor the solitary men in clubs
who drink the water of prostitution with nausea,
nor the men with a green stare
who love man and burn their lips in silence.
But against you, yes, pansies of the cities,
of tumescent flesh and unclean mind,
mud of drains, harpies, unsleeping enemies
of Love which distributes crowns of joy.

Against you always, you who give boys
drops of soiled death with bitter poison.
Against you always,
Fairies of North America,
Pájaros of Havana,
Jotos of Mexico,
Sarasas of Cadiz,
Apios of Seville,
Cancos of Madrid,
Floras of Alicante,
Adelaidas of Portugal.

Pansies of the world, murderers of doves!
Women's slaves, bitches of their boudoirs,
opened with the fever of fans in public squares
or ambushed in frigid landscapes of hemlock.

¡No haya cuartel! La muerte
mana de vuestros ojos
y agrupa flores grises en la orilla del cieno.
¡No haya cuartel! ¡Alerta!
Que los confundidos, los puros,
los clásicos, los señalados, los suplicantes
os cierren las puertas de la bacanal.

Y tú, bello Walt Whitman, duerme a orillas del Hudson
con la barba hacia el polo y las manos abiertas.
Arcilla blanda o nieve, tu lengua está llamando
camaradas que velen tu gacela sin cuerpo.
Duerme, no queda nada.
Una danza de muros agita las praderas
y América se anega de máquinas y llanto.
Quiero que el aire fuerte de la noche más honda
quite flores y letras del arco donde duermes
y un niño negro anuncie a los blancos del oro
la llegada del reino de la espiga.

Let there be no quarter! Death
flows from your eyes
and clusters grey flowers on the shores.
Let there be no quarter! Take heed!
Let the perplexed, the pure,
the classicists, the noted, the supplicants,
close the gates of the Bacchanalia.

And you, beautiful Walt Whitman, sleep on the Hudson's banks,
with your beard toward the Pole and your hands open.
Bland clay or snow, your tongue is calling for
comrades that keep watch on your gazelle without a body.
Sleep; nothing remains.
A dance of walls agitates the meadows
and America drowns itself in machines and lament.
I want the strong air of the most profound night
to remove flowers and words from the arch where you sleep,
and a black boy to announce to the gold-minded whites
the arrival of the reign of the ear of corn.

STEPHEN SPENDER
AND J. L. GILI

LLANTO POR IGNACIO SÁNCHEZ MEJÍAS

1935

LLANTO POR IGNACIO SANCHEZ MEJIAS

1. *La cogida y la muerte*

A las cinco de la tarde.
Eran las cinco en punto de la tarde.
Un niño trajo la blanca sábana
a las cinco de la tarde.
Una espuerta de cal ya prevenida
a las cinco de la tarde.
Lo demás era muerte y sólo muerte
a las cinco de la tarde.

El viento se llevó los algodones
a las cinco de la tarde.
Y el óxido sembró cristal y níquel
a las cinco de la tarde.
Ya luchan la paloma y el leopardo
a las cinco de la tarde.
Y un muslo con un asta desolada
a las cinco de la tarde.
Comenzaron los sones de bordón
a las cinco de la tarde.
Las campanas de arsénico y el humo
a las cinco de la tarde.
En las esquinas grupos de silencio
a las cinco de la tarde,
¡Y el toro solo corazón arriba!
a las cinco de tarde.
Cuando el sudor de nieve fué llegando
a las cinco de la tarde,
cuando la plaza se cubrió de yodo
a las cinco de la tarde,
la muerte puso huevos en la herida
a las cinco de la tarde.
A las cinco de la tarde.
A las cinco en punto de la tarde.

LAMENT FOR IGNACIO SANCHEZ MEJIAS

1. *Cogida and Death*

At five in the afternoon.
It was exactly five in the afternoon.
A boy brought the white sheet
at five in the afternoon.
A frail of lime ready prepared
at five in the afternoon.
The rest was death, and death alone
at five in the afternoon.

The wind carried away the cottonwool
at five in the afternoon.
And the oxide scattered crystal and nickel
at five in the afternoon.
Now the dove and the leopard wrestle
at five in the afternoon.
And a thigh with a desolate horn
at five in the afternoon.
The bass-string struck up
at five in the afternoon.
Arsenic bells and smoke
at five in the afternoon.
Groups of silence in the corners
at five in the afternoon.
And the bull alone with a high heart!
At five in the afternoon.
When the sweat of snow was coming
at five in the afternoon,
when the bull ring was covered in iodine
at five in the afternoon.
death laid eggs in the wound
at five in the afternoon.
At five in the afternoon.
Exactly at five o'clock in the afternoon.

Un ataúd con ruedas es la cama
a las cinco de la tarde.
Huesos y flautas suenan en su oído
a las cinco de la tarde.
El toro ya mugía por su frente
a las cinco de la tarde.
El cuarto se irisaba de agonía
a las cinco de la tarde.
A lo lejos ya viene la gangrena
a las cinco de la tarde.
Trompa de lirio por las verdes ingles
a las cinco de la tarde.
Las heridas quemaban como soles
a las cinco de la tarde,
y el gentío rompía las ventanas
a las cinco de la tarde.
A las cinco de la tarde.
¡Ay, qué terribles cinco de la tarde!
¡Eran las cinco en todos los relojes!
¡Eran las cinco en sombra de la tarde!

2. *La sangre derramada*

¡Que no quiero verla!

Díle a la luna que venga,
que no quiero ver la sangre
de Ignacio sobre la arena.

¡Que no quiero verla!

La luna de par en par.
Caballo de nubes quietas,
y la plaza gris del sueño
con sauces en las barreras.

¡Que no quiero verla!

A coffin on wheels is his bed
at five in the afternoon.
Bones and flutes resound in his ears
at five in the afternoon.
Now the bull was bellowing through his forehead
at five in the afternoon.
The room was iridescent with agony
at five in the afternoon.
In the distance the gangrene now comes
at five in the afternoon.
Horn of the lily through green groins
at five in the afternoon.
The wounds were burning like suns
 at five in the afternoon,
and the crowd was breaking the windows
at five in the afternoon.
At five in the afternoon.
Ah, that fatal five in the afternoon!
It was five by all the clocks!
It was five in the shade of the afternoon!

2. *The Spilled Blood*

I will not see it!

Tell the moon to come
for I do not want to see the blood
of Ignacio on the sand.

I will not see it!

The moon wide open.
Horse of still clouds,
and the grey bull ring of dreams
with willows in the barreras.

I will not see it!

Que mi recuerdo se quema.
¡Avisad a los jazmines
con su blancura pequeña!

¡Que no quiero verla!

La vaca del viejo mundo
pasaba su triste lengua
sobre un hocico de sangres
derramadas en la arena,
y los toros de Guisando,
casi muerte y casi piedra,
mugieron como dos siglos
hartos de pisar la tierra.
No.
¡Que no quiero verla!

Por las gradas sube Ignacio
con toda su muerte a cuestas.
Buscaba el amanecer,
y el amanecer no era.
Busca su perfil seguro,
y el sueño lo desorienta.
Buscaba su hermoso cuerpo
y encontró su sangre abierta.
¡No me digáis que la vea!
No quiero sentir el chorro
cada vez con menos fuerza;
ese chorro que ilumina
los tendidos y se vuelca
sobre la pana y el cuero
de muchedumbre sedienta.
¡Quién me grita que me asome!
¡No me digáis que la vea!

No se cerraron sus ojos
cuando vió los cuernos cerca,
pero las madres terribles

Let my memory kindle!
Warn the jasmines
of such minute whiteness!

I will not see it!

The cow of the ancient world
passed her sad tongue
over a snout of blood
spilled on the sand,
and the bulls of Guisando,
partly death and partly stone,
bellowed like two centuries
sated with treading the earth.
No.
I do not want to see it!
I will not see it!

Ignacio goes up the tiers
with all his death on his shoulders.
He sought for the dawn
but the dawn was no more.
He seeks for his confident profile
and the dream bewilders him.
He sought for his beautiful body
and encountered his opened blood.
I will not see it!
I do not want to hear it spurt
each time with less strength:
that spurt that illuminates
the tiers of seats, and spills
over the corduroy and the leather
of a thirsty multitude.
Who shouts that I should come near!
Do not ask me to see it!

His eyes did not close
when he saw the horns near,
but the terrible mothers

levantaron la cabeza.
Y a través de las ganaderías,
hubo un aire de voces secretas
que gritaban a toros celestes,
mayorales de pálida niebla.
No hubo príncipe en Sevilla
que comparársele pueda,
ni espada como su espada
ni corazón tan de veras.
Como un río de leones
su maravillosa fuerza,
y como un torso de mármol
su dibujada prudencia.
Aire de Roma andaluza
le doraba la cabeza
donde su risa era un nardo
de sal y de inteligencia.
¡Qué gran torero en la plaza!
¡Qué buen serrano en la sierra!
¡Qué blando con las espigas!
¡Qué duro con las espuelas!
¡Qué tierno con el rocío!
¡Qué deslumbrante en la feria!
¡Qué tremendo con las últimas
banderillas de tiniebla!

Pero ya duerme sin fin.
Ya los musgos y la hierba
abren con dedos seguros
la flor de su calavera.
Y su sangre ya viene cantando:
cantando por marismas y praderas,
resbalando por cuernos ateridos,
vacilando sin alma por la niebla,
tropezando con miles de pezuñas
como una larga, oscura, triste lengua,
para formar un charco de agonía
junto al Guadalquivir de las estrellas.

lifted their heads.
And across the ranches,
an air of secret voices rose,
shouting to celestial bulls,
herdsmen of pale mist.
There was no prince in Seville
who could compare with him,
nor sword like his sword
nor heart so true.
Like a river of lions
was his marvellous strength,
and like a marble torso
his firm drawn moderation.
The air of Andalusian Rome
gilded his head
where his smile was a spikenard
of wit and intelligence.
What a great torero in the ring!
What a good peasant in the sierra!
How gentle with the sheaves!
How hard with the spurs!
How tender with the dew!
How dazzling in the fiesta!
How tremendous with the final
banderillas of darkness!

But now he sleeps without end.
Now the moss and the grass
open with sure fingers
the flower of his skull.
And now his blood comes out singing;
singing along marshes and meadows,
sliding on frozen horns,
faltering soulless in the mist,
stumbling over a thousand hoofs
like a long, dark, sad tongue,
to form a pool of agony
close to the starry Guadalquivir.

¡Oh blanco muro de España!
¡Oh negro toro de pena!
¡Oh sangre dura de Ignacio!
¡Oh ruiseñor de sus venas!
No.
¡Que no quiero verla!
Que no hay cáliz que la contenga,
que no hay golondrinas que se la beban,
no hay escarcha de luz que la enfríe,
no hay canto ni diluvio de azucenas,
no hay cristal que la cubra de plata.
No.
¡ ¡Yo no quiero verla!!

   3. *Cuerpo presente*

La piedra es una frente donde los sueños gimen
sin tener agua curva ni cipreses helados.
La piedra es una espalda para llevar al tiempo
con árboles de lágrimas y cintas y planetas.

Yo he visto lluvias grises correr hacia las olas
levantando sus tiernos brazos acribillados,
para no ser cazadas por la piedra tendida
que desata sus miembros sin empapar la sangre.

Porque la piedra coge simientes y nublados,
esqueletos de alondras y lobos de penumbra;
pero no da sonidos, ni cristales, ni fuego,
sino plazas y plazas y otras plazas sin muros.

Ya está sobre la piedra Ignacio el bien nacido.
Ya se acabó; ¿qué pasa? Contemplad su figura:
la muerte le ha cubierto de pálidos azufres
y le ha puesto cabeza de oscuro minotauro.

Ya se acabó. La lluvia penetra por su boca.
El aire como loco deja su pecho hundido,

144

Oh, white wall of Spain!
Oh, black bull of sorrow!
Oh, hard blood of Ignacio!
Oh, nightingale of his veins!
No.
I will not see it!
No chalice can contain it,
no swallows can drink it,
no frost of light can cool it,
nor song nor deluge of white lilies,
no glass can cover it with silver.
No.
I will not see it!

3. *The Laid Out Body*

Stone is a forehead where dreams grieve
without curving waters and frozen cypresses.
Stone is a shoulder on which to bear Time
with trees formed of tears and ribbons and planets.

I have seen grey showers move towards the waves
raising their tender riddled arms,
to avoid being caught by the lying stone
which loosens their limbs without soaking the blood.

For stone gathers seed and clouds,
skeleton larks and wolves of penumbra:
but yields not sounds nor crystals nor fire,
only bull rings and bull rings and more bull rings without walls.

Now, Ignacio the well born lies on the stone.
All is finished. What is happening? Contemplate his face:
death has covered him with pale sulphur
and has placed on him the head of a dark minotaur.

All is finished. The rain penetrates his mouth.
The air, as if mad, leaves his sunken chest,

y el Amor, empapado con lágrimas de nieve,
se calienta en la cumbre de las ganaderías.

¿Qué dicen? Un silencio con hedores reposa.
Estamos con un cuerpo presente que se esfuma,
con una forma clara que tuvo ruiseñores
y la vemos llenarse de agujeros sin fondo.

¿Quién arruga el sudario? ¡No es verdad lo que dice!
Aquí no canta nadie, ni llora en el rincón,
ni pica las espuelas, ni espanta la serpiente:
aquí no quiero más que los ojos redondos
para ver ese cuerpo sin posible descanso.

Yo quiero ver aquí los hombres de voz dura.
Los que doman caballos y dominan los ríos:
los hombres que les suena el esqueleto y cantan
con una boca llena de sol y pedernales.

Aquí quiero yo verlos. Delante de la piedra.
Delante de este cuerpo con las riendas quebradas.
Yo quiero que me enseñen dónde está la salida
para este capitán atado por la muerte.

Yo quiero que me enseñen un llanto como un río
que tenga dulces nieblas y profundas orillas,
para llevar el cuerpo de Ignacio y que se pierda
sin escuchar el doble resuello de los toros.

Que se pierda en la plaza redonda de la luna
que finge cuando niña doliente res inmóvil;
que se pierda en la noche sin canto de los peces
y en la maleza blanca del humo congelado.

No quiero que le tapen la cara con pañuelos
para que se acostumbre con la muerte que lleva.
Véte, Ignacio: No sientas el caliente bramido.
Duerme, vuela, reposa: ¡También se muere el mar!

and Love, soaked through with tears of snow,
warms itself on the peak of the herd.

What are they saying? A stenching silence settles down.
We are here with a body laid out which fades away,
with a pure shape which had nightingales
and we see it being filled with depthless holes.

Who creases the shroud? What he says is not true!
Nobody sings here, nobody weeps in the corner,
nobody pricks the spurs, nor terrifies the serpent.
Here I want nothing else but the round eyes
to see this body without a chance of rest.

Here I want to see those men of hard voice.
Those that break horses and dominate rivers;
those men of sonorous skeleton who sing
with a mouth full of sun and flint.

Here I want to see them. Before the stone.
Before this body with broken reins.
I want to know from them the way out
for this captain strapped down by death.

I want them to show me a lament like a river
which will have sweet mists and deep shores,
to take the body of Ignacio where it loses itself
without hearing the double panting of the bulls.

Loses itself in the round bull ring of the moon
which feigns in its youth a sad quiet bull:
loses itself in the night without song of fishes
and in the white thicket of frozen smoke.

I don't want them to cover his face with handkerchiefs
that he may get used to the death he carries.
Go, Ignacio; feel not the hot bellowing.
Sleep, fly, rest: even the sea dies!

4. *Alma ausente*

No te conoce el toro ni la higuera,
ni caballos ni hormigas de tu casa.
No te conoce el niño ni la tarde
porque te has muerto para siempre.

No te conoce el lomo de la piedra,
ni el raso negro donde te destrozas.
No te conoce tu recuerdo mudo
porque te has muerto para siempre.

El otoño vendrá con caracolas,
uva de niebla y montes agrupados,
pero nadie querrá mirar tus ojos
porque te has muerto para siempre.

Porque te has muerto para siempre,
como todos los muertos de la Tierra,
como todos los muertos que se olvidan
en un montón de perros apagados.

No te conoce nadie. No. Pero yo te canto.
Yo canto para luego tu perfil y tu gracia.
La madurez insigne de tu conocimiento.
Tu apetencia de muerte y el gusto de su boca.
La tristeza que tuvo tu valiente alegría.

Tardará mucho tiempo en nacer, si es que nace,
un andaluz tan claro, tan rico de aventura.
Yo canto su elegancia con palabras que gimen
y recuerdo una brisa triste por los olivos.

4. Absent Soul

The bull does not know you, nor the fig tree,
nor the horses, nor the ants in your own house.
The child and the afternoon do not know you
because you have died for ever.

The back of the stone does not know you,
nor the black satin in which you crumble.
Your silent memory does not know you
because you have died for ever.

The autumn will come with small white snails,
misty grapes and with clustered hills,
but no one will look into your eyes
because you have died for ever.

Because you have died for ever,
like all the dead of the Earth,
like all the dead who are forgotten
in a heap of lifeless dogs.

Nobody knows you. No. But I sing of you.
For posterity I sing of your profile and grace.
Of the signal maturity of your understanding.
Of your appetite for death and the taste of its mouth.
Of the sadness of your once valiant gaiety.

It will be a long time, if ever, before there is born
an Andalusian so true, so rich in adventure.
I sing of his elegance with words that groan,
and I remember a sad breeze through the olive trees.

STEPHEN SPENDER
AND J. L. GILI

FROM

SEIS POEMAS GALEGOS

1935

MADRIGAL A CIBDA DE SANTIAGO

Chove en Santiago
meu doce amor.
Camelia branca do ar
brila entebrecida ô sol.

Chove en Santiago
na noite escura.
Herbas de prata e de sono
cobren a valeira lúa.

Olla a choiva pol-a rúa,
laio de pedra e cristal.
Olla no vento esvaído
soma e cinza do teu mar.

Soma e cinza do teu mar
Santiago, lonxe do sol.
Agoa da mañán anterga
trema no meu corazón.

DANZA DA LUA EN SANTIAGO

¡Fita aquel branco galán,
olla seu transido corpo!

E a lúa que baila
na Quintana dos mortos.

Fita seu corpo transido,
negro de somas e lobos.

Nai: A lúa está bailando
na Quintana dos mortos.

152

MADRIGAL TO THE CITY OF SANTIAGO

It rains in Santiago,
my sweet love.
White camellia of the air,
shadowy shines the sun.

It rains in Santiago
in the dark night.
Grasses of silver and of sleep
cover the empty moon.

See the rain in the street,
lament of stone and crystal.
See in the vanishing wind
shadow and ash of your sea.

Shadow and ash of your sea,
Santiago, far from the sun.
Water of ancient morning
trembles in my heart.

                    NORMAN DI GIOVANNI

DANCE OF THE MOON IN SANTIAGO

Regard that white gallant,
look at his spent body!

It is the moon that dances
in the Courtyard of the Dead.

Look at his spent body,
blackened with shadows and wolves.

Mother, the moon is dancing
in the Courtyard of the Dead.

¿Quén fire potro de pedra
na mesma porta do sono?

¡E a lúa! ¡E a lúa
na Quintana dos mortos!

¿Quén fita meus grises vidros
cheos de nubens seus ollos?

¡E a lúa! ¡E a lúa
na Quintana dos mortos!

Deixame morrer no leito
soñando con froles d'ouro.

Nai: A lúa está bailando
na Quintana dos mortos.

¡Ai filla, co ar do céo
vólvome branca de pronto!

Non é o ar, é a triste lúa
na Quintana dos mortos.

¿Quén brúa co-este xemido
d'imenso boi melancónico?

Nai: E a lúa, é a lúa
na Quintana dos mortos.

¡Si, a lúa, a lúa
coronada de toxos,
que baila, e baila, e baila
na Quintana dos mortos!

Who wounds the stone foal
at the very portal of sleep?

It is the moon! It is the moon
in the Courtyard of the Dead!

Who stares at my gray glasses
his eyes filled with clouds?

It is the moon! It is the moon
in the Courtyard of the Dead!

Let me perish in my bed
dreaming of golden flowers.

Mother, the moon is dancing
in the Courtyard of the Dead.

Ay, daughter, with the wind of the sky
I turn suddenly white!

It is not the wind but the sad moon
in the Courtyard of the Dead.

Who bellows with this moan
of a great melancholy ox?

Mother: The moon, it is the moon
in the Courtyard of the Dead.

Yes, the moon, the moon
crowned with furze
that dances, dances, dances
in the Courtyard of the Dead.

NORMAN DI GIOVANNI

FROM

DIVÁN DEL TARMARIT

1936

GACELA DEL AMOR IMPREVISTO

Nadie comprendía el perfume
de la oscura magnolia de tu vientre.
Nadie sabía que martirizabas
un colibrí de amor entre los dientes.

Mil caballitos persas se dormían
en la plaza con luna de tu frente,
mientras que yo enlazaba cuatro noches
tu cintura, enemiga de la nieve.

Entre yeso y jazmines, tu mirada
era un pálido ramo de simientes.
Yo busqué, para darte, por mi pecho
las letras de marfil que dicen *siempre*,

siempre, siempre: jardín de mi agonía,
tu cuerpo fugitivo para siempre,
la sangre de tus venas en mi boca,
tu boca ya sin luz para mi muerte.

GACELA DE LA TERRIBLE PRESENCIA

Yo quiero que el agua se quede sin cauce.
Yo quiero que el viento se quede sin valles.

Quiero que la noche se quede sin ojos
y mi corazón sin la flor del oro;

que los bueyes hablen con las grandes hojas
y que la lombriz se muera de sombra;

que brillen los dientes de la calavera
y los amarillos inunden la seda.

GACELA OF UNFORESEEN LOVE

No one understood the perfume
of the dark magnolia of your womb.
No one knew that you tormented
a hummingbird of love between your teeth.

A thousand Persian ponies fell asleep
in the moonlit plaza of your forehead,
while through four nights I embraced
your waist, enemy of the snow.

Between plaster and jasmines, your glance
was a pale branch of seeds.
I sought in my heart to give you
the ivory letters that say *always*,

always, always: garden of my agony,
your body elusive always,
 the blood of your veins in my mouth,
your mouth already lightless for my death.

                                          W. S. MERWIN

GACELA OF THE TERRIBLE PRESENCE

I want the water reft from its bed,
I want the wind left without valleys.

I want the night left without eyes
and my heart without the flower of gold.

And the oxen to speak with great leaves
and the earthworm to perish of shadow.

And the teeth of the skull to glisten
and the yellows to overflow the silk.

Puedo ver el duelo de la noche herida
luchando enroscada con el mediodía.

Resisto un ocaso de verde veneno
y los arcos rotos donde sufre el tiempo.

Pero no ilumines tu limpio desnudo
como un negro cactus abierto en los juncos.

Déjame en un ansia de oscuros planetas,
pero no me enseñes tu cintura fresca.

GACELA DEL AMOR DESESPERADO

La noche no quiere venir
para que tú no vengas,
ni yo pueda ir.

Pero yo iré,
aunque un sol de alacranes me coma la sien.

Pero tú vendrás
con la lengua quemada por la lluvia de sal.

El día no quiere venir
para que tú no vengas,
ni yo pueda ir.

Pero yo iré
entregando a los sapos mi mordido clavel.

Pero tú vendrás
por las turbias cloacas de la oscuridad.

I can see the duel of the wounded night
writing in battle with noon.

I resist a setting of green venom
and the broken arches where time suffers.

But do not illumine your clear nude
like a black cactus open in the reeds.

Leave me in an anguish of dark planets,
but do not show me your cool waist.

W. S. MERWIN

GACELA OF DESPERATE LOVE

The night does not wish to come
so that you cannot come
and I cannot go.

But I will go,
though a scorpion sun should eat my temple.

But you will come
with your tongue burned by the salt rain.

The day does not wish to come
so that you cannot come
and I cannot go.

But I will go
yielding to the toads my chewed carnation.

But you will come
through the muddy sewers of darkness.

Ni la noche ni el día quieren venir
para que por ti muera
y tú mueras por mí.

GACELA DEL NINO MUERTO

Todas las tardes en Granada,
todas las tardes se muere un niño.
Todas las tardes el agua se sienta
a conversar con sus amigos.

Los muertos llevan alas de musgo.
El viento nublado y el viento limpio
son dos faisanes que vuelan por las torres
y el día es un muchacho herido.

No quedaba en el aire ni una brizna de alondra
cuando yo te encontré por la grutas del vino.
No quedaba en la tierra ni una miga de nube
cuando te ahogabas por el río.

Un gigante de agua cayó sobre los montes
y el valle fué rodando con perros y con lirios.
Tu cuerpo, con la sombra violeta de mis manos,
era, muerto en la orilla, un arcángel de frío.

GACELA DE LA RAIZ AMARGA

Hay una raíz amarga
y un mundo de mil terrazas.

Ni la mano más pequeña
quiebra la puerta del agua.

Neither night nor day wishes to come
so that I may die for you
and you die for me.

W. S. MERWIN

GACELA OF THE DEAD CHILD

Each afternoon in Granada,
a child dies each afternoon.
Each afternoon the water sits down
to chat with its companions.

The dead wear mossy wings.
Winds clear and cloudy are
two pheasants in flight through the towers,
and the day is a wounded boy.

Not a flicker of lark was left in the sky
when I met you in the caverns of wine.
Not the crumb of a cloud was over ground
when you were drowned in the river.

A giant of water sprawled over the hills,
the valley tumbling with lilies and dogs.
Through my hands' violet shadow, your body,
dead on the bank, was an archangel, cold.

EDWIN HONIG

GACELA OF THE BITTER ROOT

There is a bitter root
and the world has a thousand terraces.

Nor can the smallest hand
shatter the door of water.

¿Dónde vas, adónde, dónde?
Hay un cielo de mil ventanas
—batalla de abejas lívidas—
y hay una raíz amarga.

Amarga.

Duele en la planta del pie,
el interior de la cara,
y duele en el tronco fresco
de noche recién cortada.

¡Amor, enemigo mío,
muerde tu raíz amarga!

GACELA DE LA MUERTE OSCURA

Quiero dormir el sueño de las manzanas,
alejarme del tumulto de los cementerios.
Quiero dormir el sueño de aquel niño
que quería cortarse el corazón en alta mar.

No quiero que me repitan que los muertos no pierden la sangre;
que la boca podrida sigue pidiendo agua.
No quiero enterarme de los martirios que da la hierba,
ni de la luna con boca de serpiente
que trabaja antes del amanecer.

Quiero dormir un rato,
un rato, un minuto, un siglo;
pero que todos sepan que no he muerto;
que hay un establo de oro en mis labios;
que soy el pequeño amigo del viento Oeste;
que soy la sombra inmensa de mis lágrimas.

Where are you going, where, oh where?
The sky has a thousand windows
—battle of livid bees—
and there is a bitter root.

Bitter.

The ache in the sole of the foot
is the ache inside the face,
and it aches in the fresh trunk
of night only just lopped off.

Love, my enemy,
bite your bitter root!

EDWIN HONIG

GACELA OF THE DARK DEATH

I want to sleep the dream of the apples,
to withdraw from the tumult of cemeteries,
I want to sleep the dream of that child
who wanted to cut his heart on the high seas.

I don't want to hear again that the dead do not lose their blood,
that the putrid mouth goes on asking for water.
I don't want to learn of the tortures of the grass,
nor of the moon with a serpent's mouth
that labors before dawn.

I want to sleep awhile,
awhile, a minute, a century;
but all must know that I have not died;
that there is a stable of gold in my lips;
that I am the small friend of the West wind;
that I am the immense shadow of my tears.

Cúbreme por la aurora con un velo,
porque me arrojará puñados de hormigas,
y moja con agua dura mis zapatos
para que resbale la pinza de su alacrán.

Porque quiero dormir el sueño de las manzanas
para aprender un llanto que me limpie de tierra;
porque quiero vivir con aquel niño oscuro
que quería cortarse el corazón en alta mar.

GACELA DE LA HUIDA

Me he perdido muchas veces por el mar
con el oído lleno de flores recién cortadas,
con la lengua llena de amor y de agonía.
Muchas veces me he perdido por el mar,
como me pierdo en el corazón de algunos niños.

No hay noche en que, al dar un beso,
no sienta la sonrisa de las gente sin rostro,
ni hay nadie que, al tocar un recién nacido,
olvide las inmóviles calaveras de caballo.

Porque las rosas buscan en la frente
un duro paisaje de hueso
y las manos del hombre no tienen más sentido
que imitar a las raíces bajo tierra.

Como me pierdo en el corazón de algunos niños,
me he perdido muchas veces por el mar.
Ignorante del agua, voy buscando
una muerte de luz que me consuma.

Cover me at dawn with a veil,
because dawn will throw fistfuls of ants at me,
and wet with hard water my shoes
so that the pincers of the scorpion slide.

For I want to sleep the dream of the apples,
to learn a lament that will cleanse me of the earth;
for I want to live with that dark child
who wanted to cut his heart on the high seas.

STEPHEN SPENDER
AND J. L. GILI

GACELA OF THE FLIGHT

I have lost myself in the sea many times
with my ear full of freshly cut flowers,
with my tongue full of love and agony.
I have lost myself in the sea many times
as I lose myself in the heart of certain children.

There is no one who in giving a kiss
does not feel the smile of faceless people,
and no one who in touching a newborn child
forgets the motionless skulls of horses.

Because the roses search in the forehead
for a hard landscape of bone
and the hands of man have no other purpose
than to imitate the roots below the earth.

As I lose myself in the heart of certain children,
I have lost myself in the sea many times.
Ignorant of the water I go seeking
a death full of light to consume me.

STEPHEN SPENDER
AND J. L. GILI

GACELA DEL MERCADO MATUTINO

Por el arco de Elvira
quiero verte pasar,
para saber tu nombre
y ponerme a llorar.

¿Qué luna gris de las nueve
te desangró la mejilla?
¿Quién recoge tu semilla
de llamarada en la nieve?
¿Qué alfiler de cactus breve
asesina tu cristal? . . .

Por el arco de Elvira
voy a verte pasar,
para beber tus ojos
y ponenne a llorar.

¡Qué voz para mi castigo
levantas por el mercado!
¡Qué clavel enajenado
en los montones de trigo!
¡Qué lejos estoy contigo,
qué cerca cuando te vas!

Por el arco de Elvira
voy a verte pasar,
para sentir tus muslos
y ponerme a llorar.

GACELA OF THE MORNING MARKET

Through the arch of Elvira
I want to see you pass,
to know your name
and begin weeping.

What grey moon at nine
drew the blood from your cheek?
Who gathers your seed
of sudden blazing in the snow?
What brief cactus needle
murders your crystal?

Through the arch of Elvira
I'm going to see you pass,
to drink your eyes
and begin weeping.

What voice to chastise me
you raise through the market!
What enraptured carnation
among the heaps of corn!
How far away I am near you
how near when you go away!

Through the arch of Elvira
I'm going to see you pass,
to feel your thighs
and begin weeping.

STEPHEN SPENDER
AND J. L. GILI

CASIDA DEL HERIDO POR EL AGUA

Quiero bajar al pozo,
quiero subir los muros de Granada,
para mirar el corazón pasado
por el punzón oscuro de las aguas.

El niño herido gemía
con una corona de escarcha.
Estanques, aljibes y fuentes
levantaban al aire sus espadas.
¡Ay, qué furia de amor, qué hiriente filo,
qué nocturno rumor, qué muerte blanca!
¡Qué desiertos de luz iban hundiendo
los arenales de la madrugada!
El niño estaba solo
con la ciudad dormida en la garganta.
Un surtidor que viene de los sueños
lo defiende del hambre de las algas.
El niño y su agonía, frente a frente,
eran dos verdes lluvias enlazadas.
El niño se tendía por la tierra
y su agonía se curvaba.

Quiero bajar al pozo,
quiero morir mi muerte a bocanadas,
quiero llenar mi corazón de musgo,
para ver al herido por el agua.

CASIDA DEL LLANTO

He cerrado mi balcón
porque no quiero oír el llanto,
pero por detrás de los grises muros
no se oye otra cosa que el llanto.
Hay muy pocos ángeles que canten,

CASIDA OF THE BOY WOUNDED BY THE WATER

I want to go down to the well,
I want to go up the walls of Granada,
to watch the heart pierced through
by the dark thrust of water.

The wounded boy was moaning
under his crown of rime.
Pools, cisterns, fountains
raised their swords to the wind.
What a fury of love, what a wounding edge,
such nocturnal murmurs, such a white death!
Such deserts of light were crumbling
the sands of dawn!
The boy was alone,
the city asleep in his throat.
A water spout out of his dreams
wards off the hungry algae.
The boy and his agony, face to face,
were two green rains enlaced.
The boy stretched out on the ground,
and his agony bent over.

I want to go down to the well,
I want to die my own death, by mouthfuls,
I want to stuff my heart with moss,
to watch the boy wounded by the water.

EDWIN HONIG

CASIDA OF THE LAMENT

I have shut my balcony
because I do not want to hear the weeping,
but from behind the grey walls
nothing else is heard but the weeping.
There are very few angels that sing,

hay muy pocos perros que ladren,
mil violines caben en la palma de mi mano.

Pero el llanto es un perro inmenso,
el llanto es un ángel inmenso,
el llanto es un violín inmenso,
las lágrimas amordazan al viento,
y no se oye otra cosa que el llanto.

CASIDA DE LOS RAMOS

Por las arboledas del Tamarít
han venido los perros de plomo
a esperar que se caigan los ramos,
a esperar que se quiebren ellos solos.

El Tamarít tiene un manzano
con una manzana de sollozos.
Un ruiseñor apaga los suspiros
y un faisán los ahuyenta por el polvo.

Pero los ramos son alegres,
los ramos son como nosotros.
No piensan en la lluvia y se han dormido,
como si fueran árboles, de pronto

Sentados con el agua en las rodillas
dos valles esperaban al otoño.
La penumbra con paso de elefante
empujaba las ramas y los troncos.

Por las arboledas del Tamarít
hay muchos niños de velado rostro
a esperar que se caigan mis ramos,
a esperar que se quiebren ellos solos.

there are very few dogs that bark,
a thousand violins fit into the palm of my hand.

But the weeping is an immense dog,
the weeping is an immense angel,
the weeping is an immense violin,
the tears muzzle the wind,
nothing else is heard but the weeping.

STEPHEN SPENDER
AND J. L. GILI

CASIDA OF THE BRANCHES

Along the groves of the Tamarit
the leaden dogs have come
to wait for the branches to fall,
to wait for them to break themselves alone.

The Tamarit has an apple tree
with an apple of sobs;
a nightingale hushes the sighs
and a pheasant drives them away through the dust.

But the branches are happy,
the branches are like ourselves.
They do not think of the rain and they've fallen asleep,
suddenly as if they were trees.

Seated, with water to the knees,
two valleys await the autumn.
Dusk, with the step of an elephant,
pushed aside the branches and the tree trunks.

Along the groves of the Tamarit
there are many children with veiled face
waiting for my branches to fall,
waiting for them to break themselves alone.

STEPHEN SPENDER
AND J. L. GILI

CASIDA DE LA MUJER TENDIDA

Verte desnuda es recordar la tierra
la tierra lisa, limpia de caballos.
La tierra sin un junco, forma pura,
cerrada al porvenir: confín de plata.

Verte desnuda es comprender el ansia
de la lluvia que busca débil talle,
o la fiebre del mar de inmenso rostro
sin encontrar la luz de su mejilla.

La sangre sonará por las alcobas
y vendrá con espadas fulgurantes,
pero tú no sabrás dónde se ocultan
el corazón de sapo o la violeta.

Tu vientre es una lucha de raíces
y tus labios una alba sin contorno.
Bajo las rosas tibias de la cama
los muertos gimen esperando turno.

CASIDA DE LA MUCHACHA DORADA

La muchacha dorada
se bañaba en el agua
y el agua se doraba.

Las algas y las ramas
en sombra la asombraban,
y el ruiseñor cantaba
por la muchacha blanca.

Vino la noche clara
turbia de plata mala,

CASIDA OF THE RECLINING WOMAN

To see you naked is to remember the earth.
The smooth earth, swept clean of horses.
The earth without a reed, the pure form
closed to the future: confine of silver.

To see you naked is to comprehend the desire
of the rain which seeks the feeble form,
or the fever of the sea when its immense face
cannot find the light of its cheek.

The blood will resound through the bedrooms
and arrive with flashing sword,
but you will not know where the heart
of the toad or the violet hide.

Your belly is a battle of roots,
your lips are a blurred dawn.
Under the tepid roses of the bed
the dead moan, waiting their turn.

W. S. MERWIN

CASIDA OF THE GOLDEN GIRL

The golden girl
bathed in the water
and the water turned golden.

The algae and the branches
in shadow shadowed her,
and the nightingale sang
for the white girl.

The clear night came
muddied with evil silver

con peladas montañas
bajo la brisa parda.

La muchacha mojada
era blanca en el agua
y el agua, llamarada.

Vino el alba sin mancha,
con mil caras de vaca,
yerta y amortajada
con heladas guirnaldas.

La muchacha de lágrimas
se bañaba entre llamas,
y el ruiseñor lloraba
con las alas quemadas.

La muchacha dorada
era una blanca garza
y el agua la doraba.

CASIDA DE LAS PALOMAS OSCURAS

Por las ramas del laurel
vi dos palomas oscuras.
La una era el sol,
la otra la luna.
Vecinitas, les dije:
¿Dónde está mi sepultura?
En mi cola, dijo el sol.
En mi garganta, dijo la luna.
Y yo que estaba caminando
con la tierra a la cintura
vi dos águilas de mármol
y una muchacha desnuda.

with bare mountains
under the tawny breeze.

The wet girl
was white in the water,
and the water ablaze.

The unblemished dawn came
with its thousand cow faces,
stiff and shrouded
with frozen garlands.

The girl of tears
bathed among flames,
and the nightingale wept
with charred wings.

The golden girl
was a white heron
and the water gilded her.

W. S. MERWIN

CASIDA OF THE DARK DOVES

Through the branches of the laurel
I saw two dark doves.
The one was the sun,
the other the moon.
Little neighbors, I said to them,
where is my tomb?
In my tail, said the sun.
In my throat, said the moon.
And I who was walking
with the earth at my belt
saw two eagles of marble
and a naked girl.

La una era la otra
y la muchacha era ninguna.
Aguilitas, les dije:
¿Dónde está mi sepultura?
En mi cola, dijo el sol,
en mi garganta, dijo la luna.
Por las ramas del laurel
vi dos palomas desnudas.
La una era la otra
y las dos eran ninguna.

The one was the other
and the girl was no one.
Little eagles, I said to them,
where is my tomb?
In my tail, said the sun,
in my throat, said the moon.
Through the branches of the laurel
I saw two naked doves.
The one was the other
and both were no one.

W. S. MERWIN

CHRONOLOGY

1898 Federico García Lorca is born June 5 at Fuentevaqueros, near Granada.

1918 His first book of prose, *Impressiones y Paisajes*, is published.

1920 *El Maleficio de la Mariposa*, his first play, is produced in Madrid.

1921 *Libro de Poemas*, his first book of poetry, is published.

1923 Receives his law degree at the University of Granada.

1927 His play *Mariana Pineda* is a success in Madrid; his drawings attract attention in a Barcelona art gallery.

1928 *Romancero Gitano* (*Gypsy Ballads*) is published.

1929–1930 Travels in the United States and Cuba; is poet in residence at Columbia University in New York City

1930 Upon returning to Spain his play *La Zapatera Prodigiosa* (*The Shoemaker's Prodigious Wife*) is a success in Madrid.

1931 *Canto Jondo* is published.

1933 Serves as Director of the traveling university theater, La Barraca; *Bodas de Sangre* (*Blood Wedding*) and *Don Perlimplín* are performed in Madrid; lectures in Argentina and while there directs his own plays as well as some classics in Buenos Aires.

1934 *Yerma* is produced in Madrid.

1935 The puppet play *Retablillo de Don Crissóbal* is produced in Madrid; the book of poems *Llanto por Ignacio Sánchez Mejías* is published; *Blood Wedding* (in a translation titled *Bitter Oleander*) is performed in New York City; *Doña Rosita* is first performed in Barcelona.

1936 The Falangists occupy Granada and in July they execute Federico García Lorca and throw his body in an unmarked grave.

INDEX OF TITLES AND FIRST LINES

184